Battlegroun

GERMANS AT
BEAUMONT HAMEL

Battleground series:

Stamford Bridge & Hastings by Peter Marren
Wars of the Roses - Wakefield / Towton by Philip A. Haigh
Wars of the Roses - Tewkesbury by Steven Goodchild
English Civil War - Naseby by Martin Marix Evans, Peter Burton and Michael Westaway
English Civil War - Marston Moor by David Clark
War of the Spanish Succession - Blenheim 1704 by James Falkner
War of the Spanish Succession - Ramillies 1706 by James Falkner
Napoleonic - Hougoumont by Julian Paget and Derek Saunders
Napoleonic - Waterloo by Andrew Uffindell and Michael Corum
Zulu War - Isandlwana by Ian Knight and Ian Castle
Zulu War - Rorkes Drift by Ian Knight and Ian Castle
Boer War - The Relief of Ladysmith by Lewis Childs
Boer War - The Siege of Ladysmith by Lewis Childs
Boer War - Kimberley by Lewis Childs

Mons by Jack Horsfall and Nigel Cave
Néry by Patrick Tackle
Walking the Salient by Paul Reed
Ypres - Sanctuary Wood and Hooge by Nigel Cave
Ypres - Hill 60 by Nigel Cave
Ypres - Messines Ridge by Peter Oldham
Ypres - Polygon Wood by Nigel Cave
Ypres - Passchendaele by Nigel Cave
Ypres - Airfields and Airmen by Mike O'Connor
Ypres - St Julien by Graham Keech
Walking the Somme by Paul Reed
Somme - Gommecourt by Nigel Cave
Somme - Serre by Jack Horsfall & Nigel Cave
Somme - Beaumont Hamel by Nigel Cave
Somme - Thiepval by Michael Stedman
Somme - La Boisselle by Michael Stedman
Somme - Fricourt by Michael Stedman
Somme - Carnoy-Montauban by Graham Maddocks
Somme - Pozieres by Graham Keech
Somme - Courcelette by Paul Reed
Somme - Boom Ravine by Trevor Pidgeon
Somme - Mametz Wood by Michael Renshaw
Somme - Delville Wood by Nigel Cave
Somme - Advance to Victory (North) 1918 by Michael Stedman
Somme - Flers by Trevor Pidgeon
Somme - Bazentin Ridge by Edward Hancock
Somme - Combles by Paul Reed
Somme - Beaucourt by Michael Renshaw
Somme - Redan Ridge by Michael Renshaw
Somme - Hamel by Peter Pedersen
Somme - Airfields and Airmen by Mike O'Connor
Airfields and Airmen of the Channel Coast by Mike O'Connor
In the Footsteps of the Red Baron by Mike O'Connor
Arras - Airfields and Airmen by Mikel O'Connor
Arras - Vimy Ridge by Nigel Cave
Arras - Gavrelle by Trevor Tasker and Kyle Tallett
Arras - Oppy Wood by David Bilton
Arras - Bullecourt by Graham Keech
Arras - Monchy le Preux by Colin Fox
Hindenburg Line by Peter Oldham
Hindenburg Line - Epehy by Bill Mitchinson
Hindenburg Line - Riqueval by Bill Mitchinson
Hindenburg Line - Villers-Plouich by Bill Mitchinson
Hindenburg Line - Cambrai Right Hook by Jack Horsfall & Nigel Cave
Hindenburg Line - Cambrai Flesquières by Jack Horsfall & Nigel Cave

Hindenburg Line - Saint Quentin by Helen McPhail and Philip Guest
Hindenburg Line - Bourlon Wood by Jack Horsfall & Nigel Cave
Cambrai - Airfields and Airmen by Mike O'Connor
Aubers Ridge by Edward Hancock
La Bassée - Neuve Chapelle by Geoffrey Bridger
Loos - Hohenzollern Redoubt by Andrew Rawson
Loos - Hill 70 by Andrew Rawson
Fromelles by Peter Pedersen
Accrington Pals Trail by William Turner
Poets at War: Wilfred Owen by Helen McPhail and Philip Guest
Poets at War: Edmund Blunden by Helen McPhail and Philip Guest
Poets at War: Graves & Sassoon by Helen McPhail and Philip Guest
Gallipoli by Nigel Steel
Gallipoli - Gully Ravine by Stephen Chambers
Gallipoli - Landings at Helles by Huw & Jill Rodge
Walking the Italian Front by Francis Mackay
Italy - Asiago by Francis Mackay
Verdun: Fort Douamont by Christina Holstein

Germans at Beaumont Hamel by Jack Sheldon
Germans at Thiepval by Jack Sheldon

SECOND WORLD WAR

Dunkirk by Patrick Wilson
Calais by Jon Cooksey
Boulogne by Jon Cooksey
Saint-Nazaire by James Dorrian
Normandy - Pegasus Bridge/Merville Battery by Carl Shilleto
Normandy - Utah Beach by Carl Shilleto
Normandy - Omaha Beach by Tim Kilvert-Jones
Normandy - Gold Beach by Christopher Dunphie & Garry Johnson
Normandy - Gold Beach Jig by Tim Saunders
Normandy - Juno Beach by Tim Saunders
Normandy - Sword Beach by Tim Kilvert-Jones
Normandy - Operation Bluecoat by Ian Daglish
Normandy - Operation Goodwood by Ian Daglish
Normandy - Epsom by Tim Saunders
Normandy - Hill 112 by Tim Saunders
Normandy - Mont Pincon by Eric Hunt
Normandy - Cherbourg by Andrew Rawson
Das Reich - Drive to Normandy by Philip Vickers
Oradour by Philip Beck
Market Garden - Nijmegen by Tim Saunders
Market Garden - Hell's Highway by Tim Saunders
Market Garden - Arnhem, Oosterbeek by Frank Steer
Market Garden - Arnhem, The Bridge by Frank Steer
Market Garden - The Island by Tim Saunders
Normandy - Cherbourg by Andrew Rawson
US Rhine Crossing by Andrew Rawson
British Rhine Crossing – Operation Varsity by Tim Saunders
British Rhine Crossing – Operation Plunder by Tim Saunders
Battle of the Bulge - St Vith by Michael Tolhurst
Battle of the Bulge - Bastogne by Michael Tolhurst
Channel Islands by George Forty
Walcheren by Andrew Rawson
Remagen Bridge by Andrew Rawson
Cassino by Ian Blackwell
Crete - Operation 'Merkur' by Tim Saunders

With the continued expansion of the Battleground Series a **Battleground Series Club** has been formed to benefit the reader. The purpose of the Club is to keep members informed of new titles and to offer many other reader-benefits. Membership is free and by registering an interest you can help us predict print runs and thus assist us in maintaining the quality and prices at their present levels.

Please call the office on 01226 734555, or send your name and address along with a request for more information to:

Battleground Series Club Pen & Sword Books Ltd,
47 Church Street, Barnsley, South Yorkshire S70 2AS

Battleground Europe

GERMANS AT BEAUMONT HAMEL

JACK SHELDON

Great War series editor
Nigel Cave

Pen & Sword
MILITARY

*Zur Erinnerung an die bekannten oder unbekannten Opfer der
Kämpfe an der Somme*

*In memory of all those, known and unknown, who fell during the
battles of the Somme*

First published in Great Britain in 2006 by
PEN & SWORD MILITARY
an imprint of
Pen & Sword Books Limited
47 Church Street
Barnsley
South Yorkshire
S70 2AS

Copyright © Jack Sheldon, 2006

ISBN 1 84415 443 2

The right of Jack Sheldon to be identified as Author
of this Work has been asserted by him in accordance
with the Copyright, Designs and Patents Act 1988.

A CIP catalogue record for this book is
available from the British Library

*All rights reserved. No part of this book may be reproduced or transmitted
in any form or by any means, electronic or mechanical including
photocopying, recording or by any information storage and
retrieval system, without permission from the Publisher in writing.*

Printed and bound in Great Britain by
CPI UK

Pen & Sword Books Ltd incorporates the imprints of
Pen & Sword Aviation, Pen & Sword Naval, Pen & Sword Military,
Pen & Sword Select, Pen & Sword Military Classics
Leo Cooper and Wharncliffe Books

For a complete list of Pen & Sword titles please contact:
PEN & SWORD BOOKS LIMITED
47 Church Street, Barnsley, South Yorkshire, S70 2AS, England.
E-mail: enquiries@pen-and-sword.co.uk
Website: www.pen-and-sword.co.uk

CONTENTS

List of maps 6
Introduction by the Series Editor 7
Introduction 9
Acknowledgements 11

Chapter 1 Visiting Beaumont Hamel and the Somme Battlefields 13
Chapter 2 Preliminary operations and the Capture of the
          Beaumont Hamel Area 19
Chapter 3 Development of the Defences, Mine Warfare, Patrolling
          and Raiding, Winter 1914/1915 – June 1916 33
Chapter 4 The Battle of Serre June 1915 53
Chapter 5 The Bombardment and 1 July 1916 65
Chapter 6 The Fall of Beaumont Hamel and the
          Battle for Redan Ridge November 1916 89
Chapter 7 Walks and Car Tour 105

List of Equivalent Ranks and Abbreviations 155
Organisation of German forces at Beaumont Hamel 156
Index 158

LIST OF MAPS AND DIAGRAMS

1. Area Covered by *Germans at Beaumont Hamel*, showing the sector boundaries for 1 July 1916. *p 12*
2. Defence works at the western tip of Leiling Schlucht (Y Ravine). *p 36*
3. Minefield Beaumont North – Central Area. *p 38*
4. Partial cross-section of Stollen (Mine Gallery) II Beaumont North. *p 40*
5. The route of the raid on Target Area 47 6/7 April 1916. *p 45*
6. 26th Reserve Division (North) Defences Winter 1915. *p 51*
7. Battle of Serre June 1915. Artillery and Reserves. *p 55*
8. Battle of Serre June 1915. Ground lost and gained. *p 60*
9. Mining Diagram of the Heidenkopf spring 1916. *p 62*
10. Trenches south of Beaumont Hamel 8 June 1916. *p 64*
11. Sketch of the defences of Leiling Schlucht June 1916. *p 66*
12. Defensive Fire Zones 26th Reserve Division (North) June 1916. *p 71*
13. Sketch of the Primary Points of Attack 1 July 1916. *p 73*
14. Beaumont South October 1916. *p 92*
15. Deployment of German forces Beaumont Hamel. 13 November 1916. *p 94*
16. Ground gained and lost during the Battle of the Ancre November 1916. *p 100*
17. Walk 1. Circus, Y Ravine, Newfoundland Memorial and Hawthorn Ridge. *p 107*
18. Primary and Secondary Machine Gun Positions and Arcs of Fire Beaumont South July 1916. *p 110*
19. Walk 2. Redan Ridge, Minefield, Heidenkopf and Feste Soden. *p 119*
20. Trenches Heidenkopf area June 1916. *p 122*
21. Heidenkopf Mine Craters blown on 1 July 1916. *p 129*
22. Trench Complex Serre – Feste Soden summer 1916. *p 131*
23. Car Tour. Beaumont Hamel – Beaucourt – Miraumont – Achiet le Petit – Bucquoy – Puisieux – Serre – Beaucourt Redoubt – Beaumont Hamel. *p 133*
24. German lines and route map Serre – Miraumont Sector winter 1916/17. *p 145*

INTRODUCTION BY SERIES EDITIOR

This is the first of what I hope will be a number of 'other side of the hill' accounts of the German aspects of the bitter, tenacious and often futile fighting that characterised much of the Great War. With some twenty titles in the Battleground Europe series for the 1916 Somme battle alone, it was clearly well beyond time that we had some coherent German accounts to provide the other half of the story. The problem lay in several areas: the relative paucity of accessible German primary sources, the need for a fluent German speaker who was also a capable translator and someone who was prepared to master the very difficult (for both English and modern German eyes) typeface that was in vogue when so many of the regimental accounts were produced. A further complication was that where German military records exist, the smooth, user-friendly system which so many of us know from the Public Record Office (National Archives) does not. All of these difficulties (save the last) have been overcome with the emergence on the scene of Colonel Jack Sheldon. Besides being a fluent German speaker he has the advantage of also being a professional infantryman and someone who, in his career, has spent substantial periods of time working with the German army. These are invaluable assets when writing about the Imperial German Army. The first fruits of that emerged in 2005 with The German Army on the Somme 1914 - 1916.

Thus at last we can hear something about what this remarkable military force achieved in the field in microcosm. *Beaumont Hamel* was the first of the **Battleground Europe** series to tackle a battlefield in France – in fact it was the second book in the series. The reasons for selecting it as the first site for such treatment from the British side are broadly the same as those for making it the first of the German battlefield sites to be so treated; that is to say the proximity of the unrivalled Newfoundland Memorial and the distinctive geography which makes it straightforward to trace out the action on the ground. The other factor was the survival of the great swathes of primary sources that have survived in the archives of the Bavarian and Württemberg armies – a bonus due to the federal nature of the German Empire. Now, thanks to this guide, it will be possible to study possibly the most visited site (at least by those whose ancestors served in the British Expeditionary Force) on the Western Front with a solid understanding of how the enemy fought its battles in the area of Beaumont Hamel and to be moved also by their professionalism, courage, tenacity and comradeship. Hard work has also identified a number of the casualties of the fighting here who are now buried in the German cemeteries. It is difficult not to feel the grief of their fortunate comrades who survived the war and came back in search of their graves only to find traces of so very few of them. These brave soldiers, every bit as committed as their British or French enemies, deserved a better fate than that. Hopefully this book will serve as something of a memorial for them and help us also to understand why the battles of that war were so bitterly fought.

Nigel Cave
Ngong Hills 2005

INTRODUCTION

Researching the part played by the Imperial German Army during the Great War is far from easy. The records of the Prussian army were destroyed by fire in April 1945, following a raid on Potsdam by the Royal Air Force. This meant that, at a stroke, the material relating to ninety percent of the entire German war effort disappeared. It was as though everything had vanished overnight from the Public Record Office. In addition, the terms of the Treaty of Versailles meant that all continuity of tradition was lost when Germany's historic regiments were disbanded or broken up. A researcher in the United Kingdom can call upon the resources of regimental museums and archives the length and breadth of the country in his quest for anecdotal material and photographs. His counterpart would look in vain for anything similar in Germany. There is much material in private hands, but it is a near-impossibility to access it.

However all is not lost. Many of the regiments, which opposed the British army on the Somme and elsewhere, were drawn from the south and southwest of Germany. Here archives still exist for the armies of Bavaria, Baden and Württemberg and they can be consulted. In the past few years this information has begun to be tapped and it is starting to transform our knowledge of many of these great battles – and so it should: when all is said and done, the activities of the German army make up fifty percent of the entire story. In addition many hundreds of regiments wrote their war histories between 1920 and 1939. These provide a useful source of trench-level information and interesting personal stories. They also make it clear that by the time the British army took over this sector from the French, the German army had already fought its First Battle of the Somme during the autumn and early winter of 1914. The titanic clash in the second half of 1916 was the second battle for the German army and there was to be a third when they returned to the area in the spring of 1918 – but that falls outside the scope of this book.

I have always been drawn to events in and around Beaumont Hamel. The forbears of my regiment took a terrible beating there on 1 July 1916 and then again during the Battle of the Ancre in the November of that year of appalling, attritional fighting. My search for information concerning the regiments which dealt out these blows led me to the specialist military libraries of Germany and on to the archives in

Stuttgart and Munich, where I consulted files that had never been opened in sixty years. The result of that quest is contained in this little guide, which I encourage you to use with an open mind and in a spirit of historical enquiry. At the end I hope that you will have gained an appreciation of the skill and quality of the men who, hugely outnumbered, held off a British army containing some of the finest human material that ever wore the Sovereign's uniform.

It is harder to follow the story from a German, rather than a British, point of view. The Somme of today is the battlefield of the victors of the war, but there are still traces of the German army here and there and the records are extensive. This book and its companion volume *Germans at Thiepval* are intended to complement existing **Battleground Europe** guides and to provide you with a comprehensive overview of the sector of the battlefield defended by 26th Reserve Division for two years from late September 1914 to early October 1916. Defence of Beaumont Hamel is designed to be read and used in association with the **Battleground Europe** guides *Beaumont Hamel*, *Redan Ridge*, *Serre* and *Beaucourt*, which I commend to you strongly. It is fascinating to examine the events of ninety years ago from both perspectives and I hope that this book will find a place in your glove compartment when you visit this tiny French village for which so many sacrificed so much.

Jack Sheldon
Vercors, December 2005
jandl50@hotmail.com

ACKNOWLEDGEMENTS

A number of people have helped in various ways during the production of this book. I am grateful to Lieutenant Colonel Phillip Robinson RE and Norbert Krüger for assistance with documentary material, Alex Fasse for details about *Musketen* and Andy Robertshaw for information concerning the Heidenkopf archaeological project. Chris Berrell helped by permitting me to use his photographs of the funeral of the King's Own soldier discovered during the Heidenkopf dig, as did Alistair Fraser ,who originally published the photograph associated with Jakob Hönes on his website. Stewart Mc Dermott kindly obtained the photograph of the *Musket* team and my editor Nigel Cave kept the project on the straight and narrow. I should like to express my thanks to the Wilkinsons, father Roni and son Jon, at Pen & Sword books for their layout and artwork respectively and my wife Laurie, who helped with the preparation of the maps. At Beaumont Hamel Arlene King was kindness itself; being most hospitable and allowing me once more to delve into the material archived there and Avril Williams made sure that there was a bacon sandwich waiting every time I needed one. Laurie, Arlene and Nigel shared the walks and the drive with me, making painstaking checking of detail a pleasure, whatever the weather.

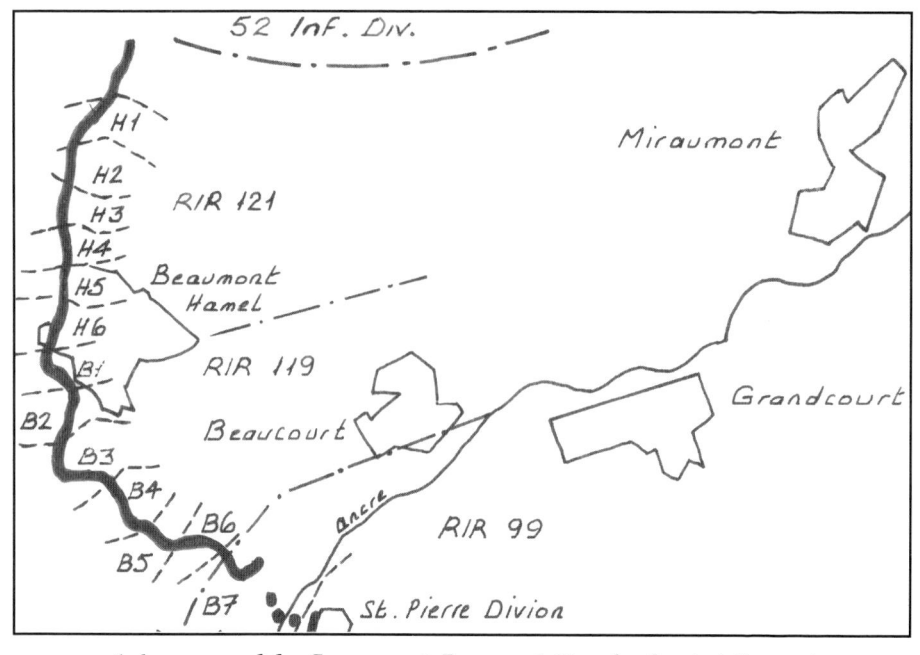

1.Area covered by Germans at Beaumont Hamel, *showing the sector boundaries for 1 July 1916*

Chapter 1

VISITING BEAUMONT HAMEL AND THE SOMME BATTLEFIELDS

General
The best advice to anyone planning to visit the Somme is to make use of the new website www.somme-battlefields.com This is an English language site, which is an initiative of the Comité du Tourisme de la Somme [Somme Tourist Board]. The site contains a mass of relevant information and is updated regularly. If you have broadband access it is possible to download several very useful and well-produced brochures, such as: 'The Visitor's Guide to the Battlefields', 'The Circuit of Remembrance' and 'The Battlefields of the Somme Visitor's Map'. Hard copies of this material are also available by applying directly to the Comité du Tourisme, 21, rue Ernest-Cauvin, 80000 AMIENS, France. Tel: +33 (0) 322 71 22 71, FAX: +33(0) 322 71 22 69, e-mail: accueil@somme-tourisme.com Armed with these items, you would have a comprehensive overview on how to plan your trip, book accommodation and obtain the best value from your visit. In addition, if you have particular questions on any aspect of the Great War or its battlefields and you wish to obtain friendly advice from an extremely knowledgeable group of enthusiasts, you should visit the Great War Forum at http://1914-1918.invisionzone.com/forums This very busy forum has about 10,000 subscribers world wide; somebody is sure to be able to answer your queries, or to point you in the right direction.

Insurance and Medical
Travel and breakdown insurance is very cheap in comparison to the potential cost of an emergency, so although you are embarking on a simple visit to a nearby EU country, rather than an expedition to the North Pole, the peace of mind obtained is probably well worth the modest outlay involved. In any event do not venture out of the UK without a European Health Insurance Card, the successor to the old E111 form. You can apply online for the card at www.ehic.org.uk or by calling 0845 606 2030. Cards take about three weeks to be delivered, but it is possible to obtain a temporary number at short notice. For those living in France it is normal to have top-up medical insurance to

complement state provision, so this is another argument for taking out some form of travel insurance, in order to ensure that you are entitled to the highest standards of treatment, should it be necessary. You will be visiting an agricultural area where there is a risk of tetanus. Make sure that your vaccination is up to date.

Independent Travellers

Most visitors from the United Kingdom tend to travel independently by car. This method probably provides the best combination of value for money and flexibility and, if you prepare carefully and bear a few straightforward rules in mind, you should have a trouble-free trip. The first point to remember is to drive on the right. This may seem obvious, but visitors from the UK are involved in accidents every year because they forget this simple fact. Danger times are first thing in the morning, or setting off after a stop for refreshments or to visit a point of interest, especially if you are on a minor, quiet country road. Put an arrow on your windscreen or have a drill to help you to remember. Carry your driving licence, log book and proof of insurance and passport at all times, but do not leave them unattended in the car. You also need a red warning triangle in case of breakdown and spare light bulbs. If you are stopped by a policeman and informed that a light is not working, production of a spare bulb from the glove compartment means that no offence has been committed.

A small first aid kit and fire extinguisher are also sensible items to carry. Make sure that you familiarise yourself with the speed limits in France (motorways 130 kph in dry weather, 110 kph in the rain; dual carriageways 110 kph; normal roads 90 kph; urban areas 50 kph, or less) and about the need to give way to traffic approaching from the right, unless you are on a priority road. Do not even think about drinking and driving. The legal limit is lower than in the United Kingdom and easily breached.

The best way to approach the battlefields of the Somme, especially if you are following the German version of events, is to arrive via the A25 or A26 and the A1 from the channel ports and to take the Bapaume exit. That way, whether you head directly down the D 929 towards Albert, or meander cross country to your destination, you will be traversing the old German rear areas, which contained all the supplies and services needed to maintain the battle in the forward battle zone. Your car will usually be filthy by the end of a tour to the Somme. There is a network of useful Eléphant Bleu coin-operated high pressure car washes in France, with a branch in Albert and an equivalent installation in Bapaume.

Accommodation

If you wish to stay close to the places discussed in this guide, you will need to book your accommodation in advance, because not much is available in or around Albert. Full details concerning places to stay is available in the literature of the Comité du Tourisme, but two addresses which are very popular with British visitors and located right in the relevant area of the battlefields are:

Julie Renshaw, Les Galets, Route de Beaumont, 80560 Auchonvillers. Tel/FAX: +33 (0)322 76 28 79

Avril Williams Guesthouse, 10 rue Delattre, 80560 Auchonvillers. Tel/FAX: +33 (0)322 76 23 66
e-mail avril@avrilwilliams.com   www.avrilwilliams.com
Avril also runs the adjoining Ocean Villas Tea Rooms which serves meals and packed lunches (prior booking is essential for coach parties).

If you find yourself with nowhere to go, call in at the Tourist Office at 9 rue Gambetta Albert, near to the Basilique. They will be pleased to help.

Useful Books

Enormous numbers of books concerning aspects of the battle of the Somme are available in print. In addition to the lengthy list of **Battleground Europe** titles, some of which: *Beaumont Hamel*, *Beaucourt*, *Redan Ridge* and *Serre*, this book is intended to complement, your attention is drawn to the following titles, which are packed with information:

The Somme Battlefields, Martin and Mary Middlebrook, Penguin Books 1994

Battlefield Guide to the Somme (Revised Edition), Major and Mrs Holt, Pen and Sword Books 2003

If you wish to learn more about the experience of warfare at trench level on the Somme from both sides of No Man's Land, then the following books will provide all the necessary reading:

The First Day on the Somme, Martin Middlebrook, Pen and Sword Books
The Somme, Peter Hart, Weidenfeld and Nicolson 2005
The German Army on the Somme 1914 – 1916, Jack Sheldon, Pen and Sword Books 2005

Maps
The maps in this book should enable you to navigate around the area following the walks and drives without problem. It is a good idea to have an up to date road atlas in the car, the excellent Major and Mrs Holt's *Battle Map of the Somme* is widely available and, if you wish to have access to the best readily available mapping, then the IGN 1:25,000 maps may be found in Arras, supermarkets in Bapaume and the Maison de la Presse adjacent to the Basilique in the centre of Albert. The area of the Somme of most interest to British visitors is covered by sheets 2407 O (Acheux-en-Amienois), 2407 E (Bapaume), 2408 O (Albert) and 2408 E (Bray-sur-Somme). They are a good investment if you wish to pursue your study of the battles further and, if you visit a point just to the north of Ovillers, you will find yourself at that soldier's nightmare, the junction of all four sheets!

Clothing and Personal Equipment
Clearly this will depend on what time of year you intend to visit. Good boots are essential for all but the simplest walks and, regardless of the season, I always take Wellingtons to wear when squelching up to distant cemeteries and points of interest. This minimises the amount of mud transferred into the car each time you get in and out. As a general rule always carry a waterproof jacket and wrap up warmly against the wind and rain in the winter. In the summer the sun can be fierce. Wear a hat and use sun screen. None of these walks is really off the beaten track, but you need to carry drinks and snacks so as to be self-sufficient. Viewing the sights of relevance to the German side of the battles requires a higher degree of effort on behalf of the visitor than do some other aspects of touring the battlefields. Much of the value is derived from gaining an appreciation of the exact placement of particular trenches and redoubts. A compass and a lightweight pair of binoculars will help you to do this. Do not forget your camera and notebook and a day sack with which to carry everything.

Refreshments
It is easier to find refreshments around Beaumont Hamel than it was up until a few years ago, but options are still fairly limited. Drinks are available at the new Visitors' Centre at the Thiepval Memorial to the Missing. Light refreshments may be obtained at the Ulster Tower, Thiepval, at the café in Beaucourt Station and at the South African Memorial at Delville Wood. More substantial meals are to be had at 'Le Tommy' Pozières, which has recently been expanded, the 'Ocean Villas'

Tea Rooms in Auchonvillers, which also supplies sandwiches to be taken away and 'Le Poppy' on the Bapaume-Albert Road at La Boisselle. There is a good quality restaurant at Authuille. This is the 'Auberge de la Vallée de l'Ancre' It is closed all day Monday and on Wednesday evenings and prior booking is advisable: Tel: 0322 75 15 18. Last and certainly not least, is the opportunity on fine days to picnic as you make you way around one of the walks. The only drawback to the plan is the fact that to buy the necessary items involves a trip to the shops in Albert or Bucquoy.

Dogs
Now that the quarantine laws have been changed, it is much easier to transport domestic animals to and from the United Kingdom and it is quite common to see dogs accompanying their owners around the battlefields. The latest rules which govern the import and export of pets may be found at: www.defra.gov.uk/animal/quarantine/index.htm.

The critical point, which travellers often get wrong and which makes the vets in Calais wealthy, is the fact that dogs arrive at the terminals not having been treated for internal and external parasites in the correct manner. They should arrive at the port in France having been treated by a vet more than 24 hours and less than 48 hours previously. Make sure when you have this done that the vet signs and dates the paperwork, adding in the time the treatment was administered. If not, the dog does not travel and it is another job for a vet in Calais, not to mention a twenty four hour delay. One veterinary practice in Albert, which you may find useful, is Delroisse- Petitprez, 16, Chemin d'Authuille. Tel: +33 (0)322 75 16 65.

Jumble demonstrates the correct drill at Beaumont Hamel cemetery.

Dogs are welcomed, or at least tolerated, in a wide range of hotels and gîtes in France, but it is as well to check in advance, unless you intend to use a chain such as Campanile/Premiere Classe www.envergure.fr or Formule 1 www.hotelformule1.com,where pets are automatically welcome. Currently there are no hotels of this type in Albert or Bapaume, but there are in places as close as Arras, Amiens, Péronne, Cambrai or Douai, all of which are convenient for the area covered by this book.

Make sure that you keep control of your animal at all times. There are very few places on the Somme where they can easily be allowed to run free, but if they walk well on a lead and you can cope with the amount of mud that they will transfer into your vehicle, they will enjoy the walks as much as you do. Be especially careful during the hunting season in the autumn. Local hunters will let fly at anything, including your dog if it is free. Note that dogs are not permitted on the site of the Newfoundland Memorial, nor is it a good idea to take them into cemeteries; use your judgement and all members of the party, including four-legged ones, will enjoy the visit.

Battlefield Debris
Modern ploughing depths and the natural action of the soil means that masses of rusting battlefield debris, including small arms ammunition, grenades, mortar bombs and shells (both conventional and chemical) appear in large quantities every year. You will frequently find such material dumped by farmers at the sides of fields awaiting collection by the démineurs who are responsible for disposing of these items safely. Leave all such items strictly alone. Do not touch or kick them; above all do not tamper with them. Even after all these years they are still lethal. Possession of live or defused items is a criminal offence in France, as is the use of metal detectors on the battlefield; so be warned.

Chapter 2

PRELIMINARY OPERATIONS AND THE CAPTURE OF THE BEAUMONT HAMEL AREA

AS A RESULT OF THE REPULSE ON THE MARNE, the withdrawal to defensive lines beyond the Aisne and the consequent stalemate in that area, the German plans for a swift decision in the West lay in tatters by September 1914. The only hope of salvaging the campaign and restoring mobility to the battlefield appeared to be to concentrate overwhelming force on the Allied left flank; a fact not lost on the Allied High Command, which was quick to introduce counter-measures. So began that phase of operations, somewhat misleadingly referred to as the 'Race to the Sea'. This certainly has more of a ring to it than a 'Race to Outflank', even though that was the truth of the matter during the autumn of that year.

The new Sixth Army under Crown Prince Rupprecht of Bavaria began offensive operations against French territorial forces rushed forward from the Amiens area to the south of the Somme region in late September. Initial checks were followed by advances conducted by I and II Bavarian Corps which faltered short of Albert. If Albert had fallen at this time, the way to Amiens would have been clear and Arras would probably have gone the same way and thus opened the routes to the channel ports to the German invaders. Much was at stake. Throughout these early hard-fought battles, in and around the important route centre of Albert, the town was seriously threatened, but never taken – French reserves were constantly moved into the area to prevent any such thing from happening. It was largely these troops who clashed with XIV Reserve Corps from Baden (28th Reserve Division) and Württemberg (26th Reserve Division), when this formation, which had spent a successful summer south of Metz, moved into battle astride the Bapaume – Albert road to take up the fight to the north of the Bavarians.

Following an exhausting seventy-hour train journey, XIV Reserve Corps was concentrated at Cambrai on 27 September 1914 and, after a short pause, pushed forward to Bapaume, which was taken without a fight. Orders for the further advance on Albert were given out by the commander of the 26th Reserve Division by the French memorial, erected to mark the Battle of Bapaume in January 1871 and, by 9.00 pm, the divisional advance guard, Reserve Infantry Regiment (RIR) 119, had reached the sugar refinery at Courcelette. Coming under fire from two companies of the French 22nd Territorial Regiment, who were in hasty defence in Pozières, the regiment put in an immediate two-battalion night attack, forced the French troops out and occupied the village.

28 September was a day of hard fighting for the 26th Reserve Division. Its objective was Albert, but it failed to get there, being halted along the line of the Ancre, despite having taken Thiepval, Ovillers and La Boisselle. French resistance increased with each passing hour and, despite a valiant effort and at the cost of serious casualties, the overall German advance was beginning to stall yet again. Whilst Infantry Regiment 180 and Reserve Infantry Regiments 119, 120 and 121 were fully committed to the attack that day, Reserve Infantry Regiment 99, which hailed from Mönchengladbach in the Rhineland and was thus the only regiment of 26th Reserve Division which did not come from Württemberg, was following up in reserve. It arrived in the Cambrai area on 27 September, its 2nd and 4th Battalions having detrained previously in Denain and Lourches respectively then, on 28 September, it assembled under its commander in Fontaine Notre-Dame and set out in the early morning as a formed formation along the Roman road towards Bapaume and Albert. It intended to cover thirty kilometres that day, relying, because of an interruption in supply, on food and forage requisitioned along the way.

In order to secure these items, the commander directed that herds of cattle were to be gathered in from fields left and right of the route and to be driven forward with the regiment. He also sent a supply officer forward in a motorised vehicle to Bapaume to demand and, if necessary, seize large quantities of bread, wine and fodder. It is not completely clear how successful he was, because numerous French and German units had already passed this way. Nevertheless there were extensive seizures of arms and ammunition from lightly wounded French soldiers and he also came across large numbers of French topographical maps of the area, which were to prove extremely valuable in the days to come.

The advance of the regiment was marked by the sight of burning farms in all directions and many groups of French wounded. By around midday it arrived at Bapaume where it was fed, had a break and left its heavy baggage behind. When it set out, it was split into its constituent parts and deployed in attack formation because of the proximity of the

Light field howitzer of RFAR 26 hastily dug in, autumn 1914.

enemy. 3rd Battalion, less 2nd Company, which was detached to Beaulencourt, but reinforced by 7th Company, advanced to the northwest edge of Irles and occupied positions facing northwest. 2nd and 4th Battalions advanced along the main road to Albert, passing through Le Sars and continuing on to Courcelette. The 4th Battalion spent the night there with Headquarters 7th Cavalry Division, but because of the need to secure crossings over the Ancre, the 2nd Battalion was ordered forward to secure the more northerly crossings at Grandcourt and Miraumont. Screened by cavalry and a jäger cycle company, the 2nd Battalion advanced through light and ineffective shrapnel fire to make contact with Infantry Regiment (IR) 180 on the left in the Thiepval area and its own 3rd Battalion on the right and arrived in Miraumont without casualties.

Here it came under fire from high explosive shells, but the fire was badly directed. Having relieved the jäger company at Beauregard Farm, forward of Miraumont, the battalion pulled back to the edge of the village and dug in hastily, leaving listening posts forward. A search of the village yielded a few French prisoners, one of whom was a sergeant major who was carrying his company funds with him. (It is not known what happened to the money.) The field kitchens were then brought forward so that the troops could be fed a hot meal. The battalion passed

Beauregard Farm in autumn 1914, before its destruction.

a quiet night and prepared to continue the advance on to the high ground to the northwest the following day. Heavy French artillery fire and attacks put paid to that idea, however. Far from yielding to German pressure, the French launched a series of attacks against 3rd Battalion throughout the day, in an attempt to re-cross the Ancre. The main attacks were launched in the early morning, then again in the afternoon and evening, but so well was the German artillery handled that only Krausch's platoon from 10th Company was directly involved in a fire fight with the French that day.

Grandcourt had been put in a state of defence by 2nd Battalion, with the main front facing north, where there was good observation and good fields of fire. There was, however, some concern that covered approaches from the direction of Beaucourt meant that there was a risk of a flanking attack and, sure enough, at about 9.00 am, the French launched a four company (up to 1,000 men) attack. One company approached from the north and three from the area around Beaucourt. Because these manoeuvres were identified promptly, the German artillery, working in close association with the defending companies, easily defeated this attempt. Nevertheless that was just a probing effort. At around 2.00 pm, a second attack, this time in about twelve company strength (about 3,000 men) was launched in a determined manner. Two platoons (about 150 men) from the 10th Company in Miraumont had been moved to Grandcourt in a counter-attack role, but they did not intervene. The firepower of 5th Company and outstanding support from the guns of 26 Reserve Field Artillery Regiment, operating from covered positions on Hill 133, 1,200 metres west southwest of Pys, shot this attack, too, to a standstill and drove it back with heavy losses. The 4th Battalion, which had double marched forward into what later became known as the Stallmulde/Baummulde (Stable Hollow-Boom Ravine) area, was not required immediately either, but remained where it was in reserve.

The situation along the entire XIV Reserve Corps front remained unclear and extremely tense. To the southwest German troops had pulled back to go firm along the line of the Thiepval ridge. Here around Grandcourt there remained undiminished threats from both north and west and there were wide gaps between the regiments everywhere. That evening, at around 7.00 pm, a further attack was signalled when the guns on Hill 133 came under heavy artillery fire from the Beaumont Hamel area. So as to be best placed to control events, the commander of RIR 99, Oberst Grall, moved forward to Grandcourt, together with the 13th and 16th Companies which reinforced the village itself. The night was spent improving positions and 10th Company was inserted into the line to the left of the 6th Company so as to extend the defended area. The 13th Company was put under command of the 2nd Battalion and 14th and 15th Companies under Major Freiherr Gerhard von Meerscheidt-Hüllessem, the commanding officer of 3rd Battalion, who called them forward to Miraumont.

That night the regiment achieved a minor, but locally important, success. The 7th Company had carried out a reconnaissance in the direction of Beauregard Farm, a locality which had been evacuated

French prisoners captured during the taking of Miraumont, September 1914.

earlier. This established that the area was occupied by a headquarters and a complete French battalion. Once the news reached Reserve Field Artillery Regiment 26, its 1st Battalion opened fire on the farm with great effect. The garrison fled leaving, according to a French soldier captured the following day, 100 dead and 200 wounded behind. The situation was little changed during the next few days. The French continued to attack determinedly, reconnaissance was pushed out vigorously, the positions were strengthened, there was much artillery fire and the infantry exchanged fire at relatively long range.

Meanwhile the front began to extend to the north and the French brought down large amounts of artillery fire. Thanks to their well-chosen positions, the regiment suffered very few casualties, but there was a lot of damage in Grandcourt. The church was badly damaged and five civilian inhabitants were killed. Most of the fire seemed to be coming from Serre, Puisieux and Beaumont Hamel. Despite being outnumbered, the German guns gave a good account of themselves. On 1st October, for example, the French attacked yet again near to Beauregard Farm, but were engaged so effectively by the guns, that 7th Company, advancing rapidly, was able to capture 120 members of the 18th Territorial Regiment.

Because of fears that French manoeuvring would lead to the advanced elements of XIV Reserve Corps being outflanked, on 2nd October the Guard Corps, newly arrived, launched an attack on its right flank via Achiet le Petit towards Puisieux and Serre. All through 3rd October the progress of the attack was monitored anxiously, so as to seize the first opportunity of continuing the advance. Towards evening there were signs that French pressure against the right flank was beginning to ease somewhat and elements of the 4th Battalion, less 13th Company that was in Grandcourt, advanced and dug in to the northeast of Beauregard Farm. The following day, Saturday 4th October 1914, the 4th Battalion, with 9th Company following up, advanced towards the Ruined Mill and occupied positions which would facilitate an attack on Beaucourt. As they neared their objective they came under heavy fire, but because they were using a spread out artillery formation, there were hardly any casualties. Major Rettburg, the commander, was wounded by shrapnel at this time. He handed over command to Hauptmann Bretthauer, but remained for the time being with the battalion. That night the battalion dug in. Contact was established with 2nd Battalion on its left and the Guard Corps on its right. Information arrived from Division that the French were withdrawing in the face of pressure from the Guards and that friendly troops further north were also making progress.

The information was accompanied by new grouping instructions and orders. RIR 99, reinforced by elements of RIR110 and 4th Company Engineer Battalion 13, with 1st Battalion RFAR 26 in support, was to attack and gain the line: Heights East of Beaumont – Ancre Crossing southwest of Beaucourt by the evening of 5 October. This was an ambitious plan, which involved an advance of around 3,000 metres, demanded careful planning and swift, vigorous execution. By 2.00 am on 5 October, the regiment had begun a night advance with two battalions in a line: left, 2nd Battalion, right 4th Battalion. The 2nd Company was to follow up in support of the right flank. To keep the right flank strong, Major von Meerscheidt-Hüllessem, a very experienced and forceful officer, was put in command of the 9th and 12th Companies and 6th Company RIR 110 followed up, echeloned to the right behind his force for purposes of flank protection. He set off promptly with 9th Company right and 12th Company left, both moving in company columns and headed directly in a bold right hook for Beaumont Hamel. The troops made good progress, manoeuvring confidently through unfamiliar terrain onto the high ground northeast of Beaumont Hamel, coming under artillery fire and driving off weak French defending forces before deploying into attack formation and carrying the high ground around Redan Ridge in one great charge.

With surprise on his side, by 5.30 am Reserve Leutnant G. Müller with about thirty men had forced a way daringly into Beaumont Hamel itself. All the buildings were searched and about fifty unwounded French soldiers were taken prisoner. The attackers just succeeded in preventing a fully loaded ammunition wagon from escaping and a dressing station, with fifty wounded men and medical staff, was also captured. Vizefeldwebel Schleicher arrived with a further three sections at the southern end of the village, drove back some entrenched French infantrymen, joined forces with Leutnant Müller and the entire platoon deployed into line and pushed on westwards in the direction of Auchonvillers. Having arrived on Hawthorn Ridge, however, Müller observed that a French battalion was

Major Freiherr (Baron) Gerhard von Meerscheidt-Hüllessem, a battalion commander with RIR 99 and the man who led the capture of Beaumont Hamel in October 1914.

Midday meal in a forward trench, autumn 1914.

assembling near the village. He directed volleys of small arms fire onto the first company, which caused it to pull back into the shelter of the houses and farms of Auchonvillers. The other two companies attempted to continue the advance, but were beaten back by the Germans on Redan Ridge.

Major von Meerscheidt-Hüllessem had gathered together about thirty men and sent them forward to bolster his firing line. A very difficult morning followed for the German soldiers. Two French batteries came into action in support of their infantry, it was not possible to pass a message back reporting the unexpectedly simple capture of Beaumont Hamel and, as a result, up until midday Meerscheidt-Hüllessem's men were subjected to heavy and accurate German artillery fire which was designed to soften up the non-existent French defenders of the village. Mounting casualties forced the forward platoon to seek shelter in the cellars of the farm buildings on the northern edge of the village, but they hung on, reinforced by men who could be spared from elsewhere, maintaining a grip on the village until, at around 4.00 pm, a small number of reinforcements (about seventy) from RIR 110 led by the commander himself, arrived. Further troops, drawn from Bavarian Infantry Regiments 5 and 17 were also rushed forward, so by the evening of 5 October Beaumont and the surrounding heights were firmly in German hands. The taking of Beaumont Hamel in this manner was a first class feat of arms and RIR 99 was rightly proud of its performance.

Setting off also at 2.00 am and divided from the half battalion which had headed for Beaumont Hamel, the 4th Battalion moved against the high ground to the north of Beaucourt. By 4.00 am it was in an assault position along the line of the road Beaucourt-Serre and threatening to outflank the defenders but, under pressure from the 3rd Battalion and elements of RIR 110, some of the defenders withdrew. The 4th Battalion dug in astride the road and spent the remainder of the day holding their positions and taking a certain number of casualties from artillery fire. From its left flank 13th and 14th Companies became involved in the fight for Beaucourt which, despite the success at Beaumont Hamel, was the critical part of the French position in this area. The chateau high above it offered superb fields of fire for French machine guns and all the entrances to the village, which was by now fortified on all sides, had been barricaded. The assault on the village itself was entrusted to 2nd Battalion, which advanced with

Commander and staff of 2nd Battalion RIR 99 in December 1914.

5th and 8th Companies forward and 7th Company in reserve on the left flank.

All went according to plan until the leading companies were within 300 metres of the village, when they were engaged by a torrent of fire. Using fire and manoeuvre the 8th Company, under the command of Reserve Leutnant Robert Mechenbier, closed up on the edge of the village. Despite the storm of fire directed against them, the attackers, with shouts of *'Hurra!'*, closed up to grenade-throwing range, then forced an entry into the built up area. With their veteran regimental commander, Oberst Grall, hard on their heels, the leading waves began fighting through the village from house to house. Engineers under Hauptmann Neininger were on hand to blow up obstacles and open the way through walls, until gradually the 8th Company had forced a way as far as the western edge, where it was checked by heavy fire. The noise of intense fighting could be heard from the direction of the chateau, where enemy machine gunners were still conducting a desperate defence.

At the southern end of the village, 5th Company was involved in a deadly fire fight down by the railway embankment and was unable to make further progress. The 8th Company had to take up the assault once more. Relieved at the western edge by elements of 4th Battalion, the 8th moved cautiously to the centre of the village. Reinforced by the engineers and half of 14th Company, it launched an attack on the final defended barricade. By 6.30 am resistance slackened and 13th Company drove the final defenders from the garden of the chateau. Later in the day 6th and 10th Companies were pushed forward to secure Beaucourt Station and the Ancre Valley. That evening the field kitchens came forward with much needed hot food, gifts from home and the first mail that had arrived in a long time. As night fell, the sound of artillery fire died away, to be replaced by the sound of picks and spades as the gains were consolidated. As dawn broke on 6 October, both Beaucourt and Beaumont Hamel came under very heavy artillery fire. There was no question of continuing to dig defensive positions; all except essential sentries were forced to take cover wherever it was available. French troops filtered back into Hamel and Authuille, pursued by German fire, whilst men of RIR 119 moved into Saint Pierre Divion.

3rd Battalion RIR 99 consolidated in the village of Beaumont Hamel, two companies of 4th Battalion dug in along Y Ravine, two others on the high ground of Hawthorn Ridge, whilst the 2nd Battalion took up positions all the way down to the Ancre. In addition to

The first rudimentary trenches and dugouts appear: late 1914.

beginning to dig in, elements of 2nd Battalion attempted to push forwards southwest. The commander, Major Richard Laue, took a few cyclists and conducted a reconnaissance in person in the direction of Hamel, but was checked by fire from a platelayer's shed before the village. Following up, 6th Company under Landwehr Oberleutnant Vonnegut captured the position and pushed on towards Hamel. Unfortunately, at a critical moment, French children were in the line of fire. There is no suggestion that the French soldiers had used them as human shields, but nevertheless the German attackers ceased fire until they could be rescued. Although they went on to occupy the southern outskirts of the hamlet, the impetus had gone out of the attack. Reinforced during the night by a platoon of 10th Company under Reserve Leutnant Krausch, they attempted to hold this extremely exposed position, but to no avail. It was overlooked from the high ground to the south and southwest of Hamel and it proved to be impossible to advance further against well-directed artillery fire. 5th Company tried, but was driven back. It was already clear that the Germans lacked the strength to advance any further.

Beaumont Hamel winter 1914 – 1915; already damaged by the initial battles.

Men of RIR 99 take a pause during on the early excavations at Y Ravine in the autumn of 1914.

The 6th Company was directed to withdraw and it pulled back along a covered route to the east of the railway embankment. The French accepted tacitly that a further assault by them was, for the time being, out of the question and they established a strong defensive position along the line Auchonvillers – Mesnil. Hamel was re-occupied on 7 October and, after advancing cautiously, the French dug in about 200-400 metres short of the new German line. For the time being troops from RIR 110 were retained in the area. Oberst Grall was temporarily made a brigade commander, responsible for the defence from the northern end of Redan Ridge on the Serre-Mailly road down to the Ancre and Major Laue assumed command of RIR 99.

During the coming days work went ahead at a furious pace. The artillery moved forward into positions in the so-called Artillery Hollow north of Beaucourt and a draft of 1,800 men arrived from Alsace as regimental reinforcements. Although a high proportion of the men of RIR 99 hailed from the Rhineland, from Mönchengladbach, Krefeld

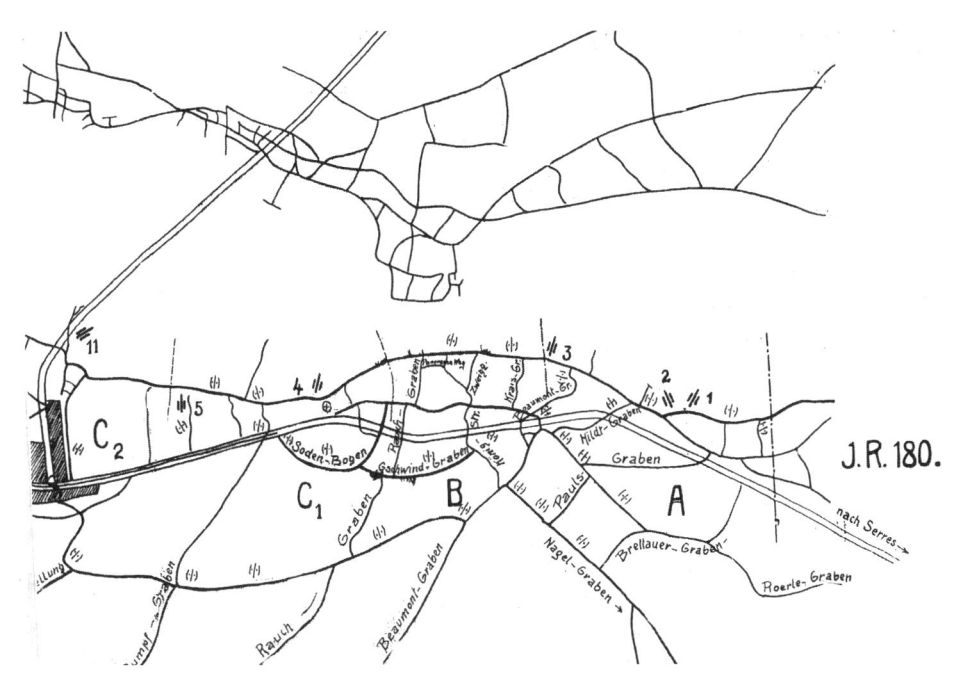

2. Opposing trench lines on Redan Ridge early 1915. Notice how close together they are in the centre. This section of the crest was constantly disputed through mining and counter-mining.

and Dusseldorf, the regiment actually mobilised in Strasbourg and Zabern, calling up reservists from Alsace to make up the numbers. The defences around Beaucourt and Beaumont Hamel developed rapidly. The first wire obstacles were placed, dugouts were produced, walls were loopholed and windows and doors barricaded as the buildings were turned into fortresses. Trenches began to snake in all directions, connecting buildings and linking up with the high ground. Finally the Ancre was bridged in several places. In general the days were quiet, but as well as the work on the defences, there were clashes most nights between patrols and concentrations of fire against known positions. Beaumont Hamel suffered in particular in this way. As a result there was a constant stream of casualties in the early days until reliance on the protection afforded by thin-walled farm buildings was replaced by the general use of dugouts. It was clear within a few days that stalemate had been reached here, too, at the most westerly point of the advance of XIV Reserve Corps and the two sides settle down to a lengthy period of trench warfare.

Chapter 3

DEVELOPMENT OF THE DEFENCES, MINE WARFARE, PATROLLING AND RAIDING WINTER 1914/1915 – JUNE 1916

IN GENERAL THE SOMME was a quiet part of the Western Front, at least until the British took over in the summer of 1915, but efforts never ceased to improve the positions, to dominate No Man's Land and to conduct offensive and defensive mining operations to the limit of the means available. Very quickly the village of Beaumont Hamel was fortified and trench lines began to appear on all dominating heights nearby. During the first winter of the war there were still gaps which could only be covered by artillery fire or patrols but, as the months went by, the defences became more and more formidable and the living accommodation improved out of all recognition. During these early months the sector was the responsibility of RIR 99 under Oberst Grall. Under his firm leadership rapid progress was made. This was just as well; the failure to advance onto the Auchonvillers ridge in October 1914, meant that this sector was overlooked and particularly vulnerable to artillery fire, especially during the period when the defences were restricted to one single trench line. The chalk was hard to dig, but it did permit the construction of extremely sound trenches, dugouts and tunnels. One of Grall's officers, Hauptmann Leiling, who commanded 14th Company of 4th Battalion, was particularly adept at this work.

On Redan Ridge the lines were particularly close together and both sides worked constantly to gain an advantage. Very soon the war disappeared underground as miners from both sides struggled for dominance. The French blew the first mines as a diversion for a major assault on Ovillers on 17 December 1914 and thereafter the battle continued ceaselessly in the area to the west of the present-day locations of Redan Ridge Cemeteries Numbers 1 and 3. Once the British engineers arrived, there was further intensification of activity. The German defensive gallery dug forward of and parallel to their front line was effective, but never succeeded in sealing off all British attempts to blow mines. In January 1916 there was a flurry of activity, with a German explosion on 2 January, followed a week later by explosions on the 8th and 9th, which checked the British miners, but

Driving the mine gallery of the Schlucht Stollen (Ravine Mined Dugout) forward into the western tip of Y Ravine.

not for long. British camouflets fired on the 16th, 17th and 18th blew in a fifteen metre length of the German gallery, but there were no casualties. The mining continued day and night. Mines and camouflets were blown by the two sides successively on the 24th and 27th January, followed by others on the 4th, 21st and 25th February, but to no great effect. The British and German trench garrisons came to regard the activity as almost routine and the German defensive gallery served as an effective barrier to a surprise attack on the main position. Then on the 2nd March, there was an altogether more nerve-wracking incident for the men of Reserve Infantry Regiment 119 and their supporting engineers.

For several days we had heard a pair of enemy miners at work, so the charging of a half-complete mine chamber was ordered. The carriers laboured to move the anonymous boxes, which concealed death. Slowly the chamber was filled. The work was punctuated by listening pauses. The charge was almost complete. Suddenly, what was that? There was no sound, no thuds any more. Had the British sensed the danger and suspended the work? Suddenly the engineer manning the listening apparatus felt the blood rushing into his head. The temperature underground seemed to have become unbearable. Oh God! The British are loading. The equipment

HAUPTMANN FRANZ LEILING. He was posted into RIR 99 at the outbreak of war from Infantry Regiment 136 as an Oberleutnant and became the regimental adjutant, but not for long. He took over command of 14th Company after Hauptmann Hofrichter was wounded on 21 August 1914. The majority of the regiment were miners or workers from other large concerns in the northern Rhineland. Some were from Baden and around 1,000 were from Alsace. It had been operating with 26th Reserve Division since August 1914. It is not known if Leiling had any background in mining, but he was obviously a good organiser, because he was responsible for the development of the complex dugouts in and around *Leilingschlucht* (Y Ravine), including the *Schluchtstollen* (Ravine Dugout) at the western tip of Y Ravine and the *Leilingstollen* (Leiling Dugout) in B4, which was served by a light railway. The *Verkehrstunnel* (Traffic Tunnel), parallel to Station Road and the major tunnel complex in St Pierre Divion were also projects of his. The works in St Pierre Divion were surveyed by the Royal Engineers after capture in November 1916. They estimated that they would hold 300 men immediately and up to 1,000 if some clearance work was undertaken. Leiling was killed in later fighting at Cambrai on 2 October 1918, having given good service and having commanded both the 4th and the 3rd Battalions RIR 99 at various times.

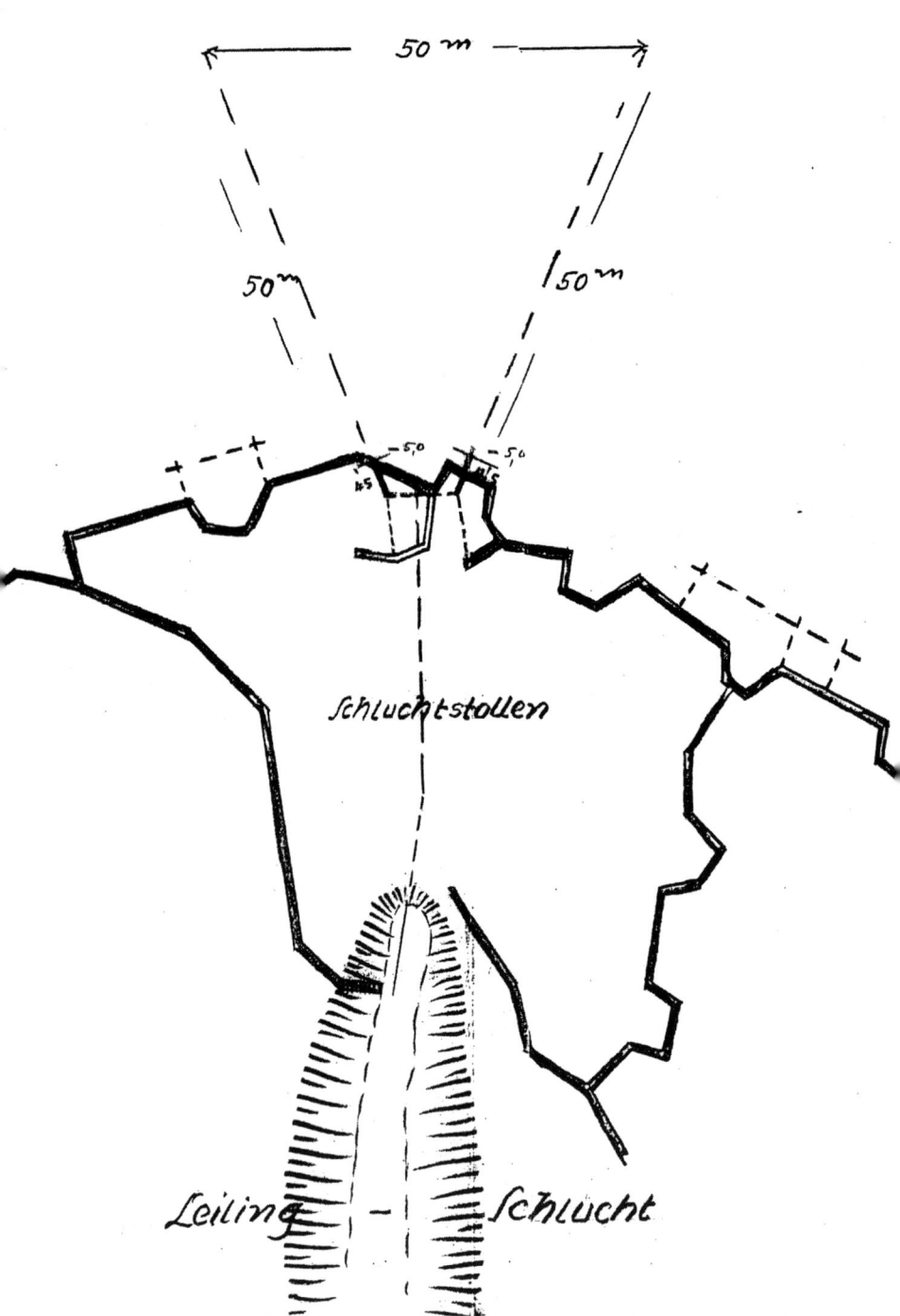

2. Sketch of the defence works at the western tip of Y Ravine and the line of the Schlucht Stollen (Ravine Mined Dugout)

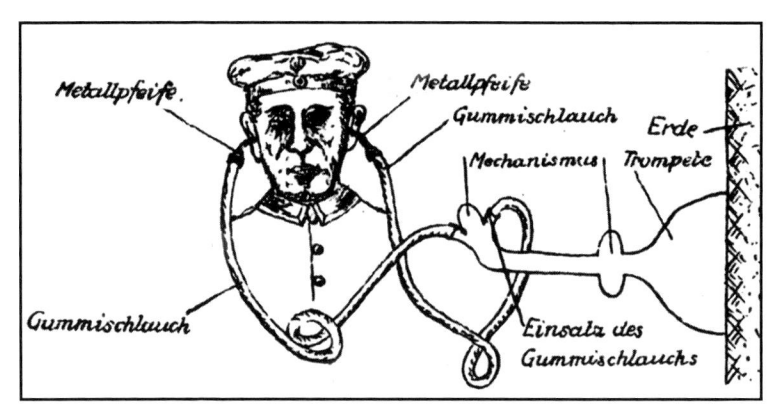

An illustration of British listening equipment used in mine galleries taken from a contemporary intelligence report. Listening for too long cannot have been good for you, if the expression of the model is anything to go by.

amplified the rustling which must have been coming from the movement backwards and forwards. Now it had become a life or death race. Swiftly the loading was completed. The detonators were placed and the firing cables were run out. Now began the work of tamping. Sandbags and beams were used to block the gallery back: five, ten, twenty metres. The overpressure from exploding gases is terrible. Insufficient tamping is a disaster, because the material is flung out in a terrible spray which blows back into our own mine system and trenches.

Now night had fallen. Still the work went on at a feverish pace. Up above the night sentries were coming on duty. Flares shot up into the sky like meteorites, before falling down to extinguish themselves in the enemy wire obstacle. Patrol activities began in the neighbouring sectors, but it was quiet today in the minefield. Here death lay in wait. The clock moved on towards midnight. The mine gallery is charged and ready for firing. One of the engineers informs the company commander. The soldiers manning the trench know what they have to do. The artillery stands by ready to fire. The engineer leutnant sits in a dugout and connects the firing cables to a small four-cornered box. Carefully he tests the circuit and the trembling magnetic needle protrudes. A sapper mounts the dark stairs and reports that everything is ready to fire and that all the galleries and shafts have been cleared of workers.

Slowly the officer withdraws the spring – loaded firing mechanism out of the box. His watch lies in front of him. The blast

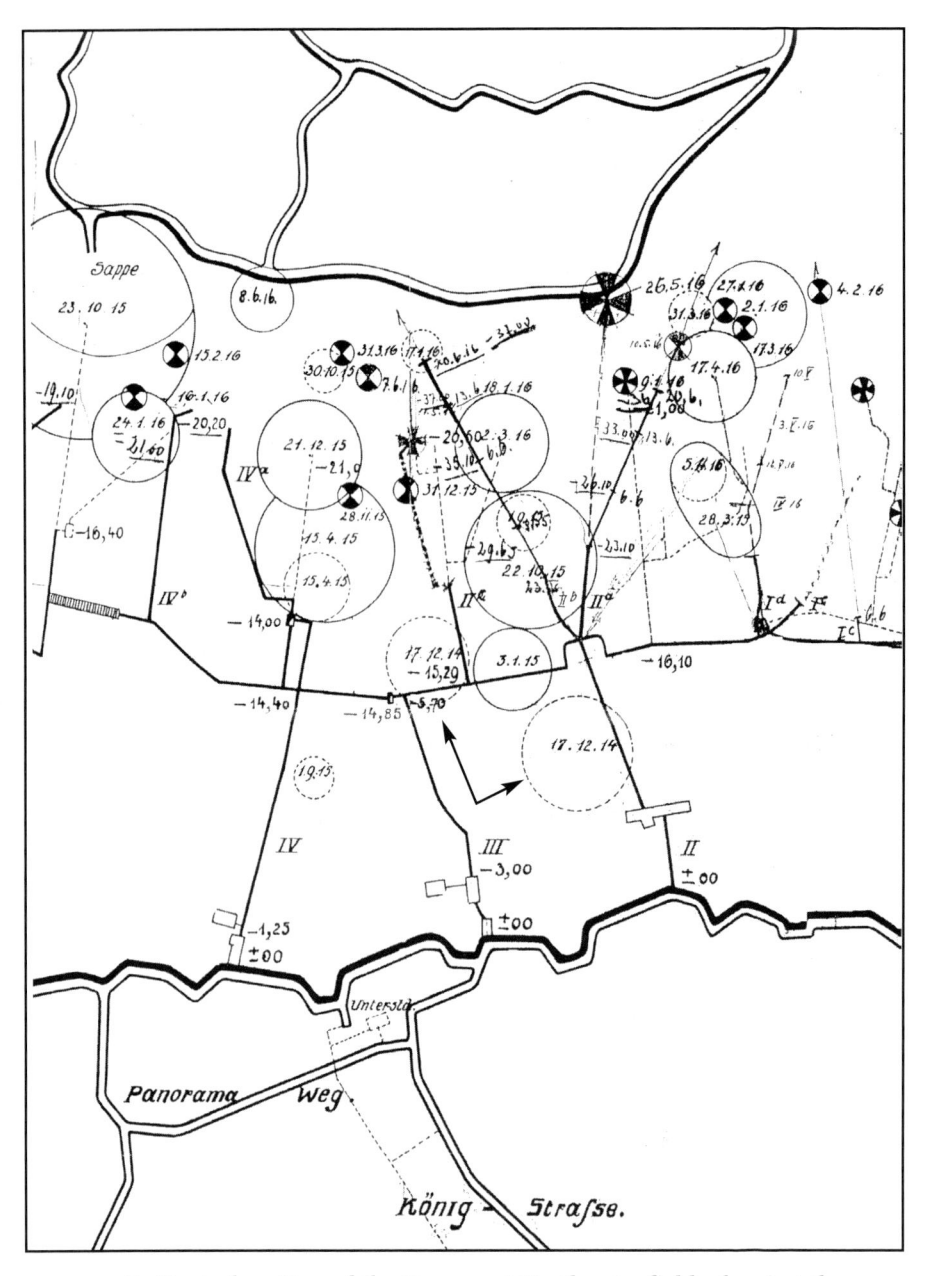

3. Central section of the Beaumont North minefield, showing the position of the various mine craters. Note the French craters of 17 December 1914, which were amongst of the first to be blown on the Western Front.

is scheduled for exactly midnight. Outside and to the sides of the site of the explosion, a hundred eyes bore into the night; calloused, cramped hands grip cold weapons; mortars and earth mortars await the instant when they can launch their bombs into the enemy trenches, which following the shock of the explosion will be filled with enemy troops. Midnight! The button is pressed! The clockwork mechanism in the box whirs. All the lights go out. The dugout sways and threatens to collapse. The very earth quakes. The ground heaves up like a wave above the seat of the explosion and falls back once more. A light cloud of dust seems to be hovering over the site. Suddenly blue flames rush skywards out of a crater, dancing and flickering on the ground and roaring upwards into the sky. This lasts for several seconds! Over there in the enemy trench, two long blue flames like snakes' tongues, lunge forwards seeking victims. No Man's Land is lit up by this ghostly light. Shots crash out. A machine gun starts to chatter. Can we hear shrieks?

A well-constructed and revetted front line trench in the Beaumont North minefield.

Total darkness descends once more! On the eastern horizon flashes can be seen and then comes the howl of howitzer shells boring down and exploding on the British lines.The murderous bombs of the mortars and earth mortars shoot up in the air like rockets, their trajectories marked like meteors in the sky. A vision of hell unfolds. The fire concentration lasts for five minutes then everything is quiet. What has happened? Apparently the enemy had also prepared a charge. We had fired ours first and the explosion had blown his charge violently to the rear. For two weeks all was quiet in the minefield.

Throughout 1915 patrol activity had been constant along the brigade front. Critical lessons were learned and applied so, by the early months

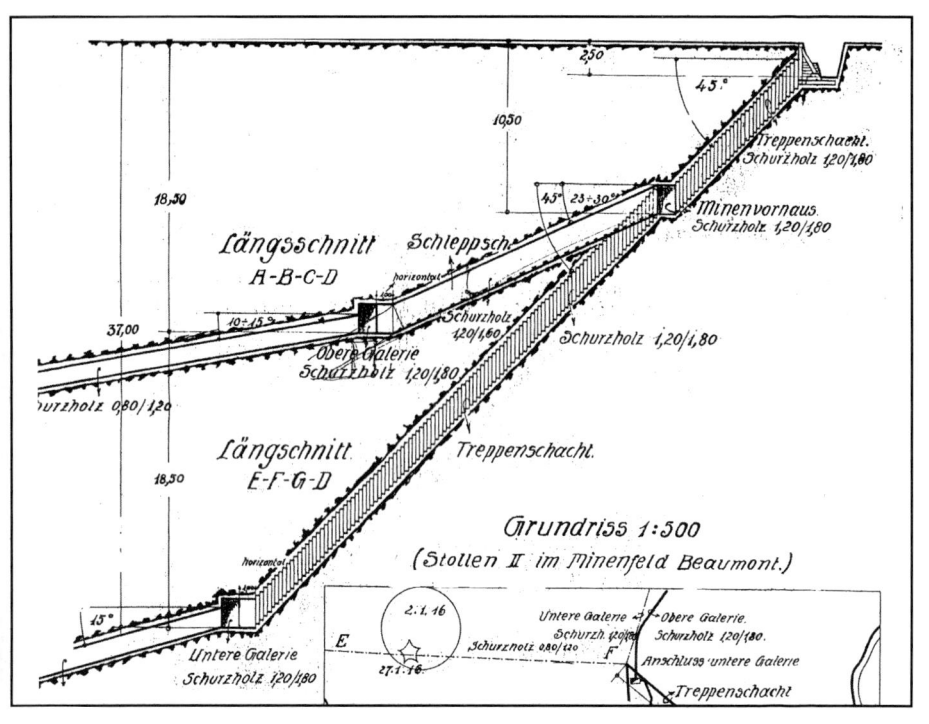

4. Partial cross-section of Stollen II (Mine 2) in the Beaumont Minefield. This shows clearly the two levels of working which were pushed forward and the dimensions of the main galleries (1.2 x 1.80 metres)

of 1916, the units of XIV Reserve Corps were conducting highly sophisticated and frequently successful raids. One such was conducted by Major von Ellrichhausen's 2nd Battalion Reserve Infantry Regiment 119 on Target Area 47 in the Beaumont Hamel area near Y Ravine, during the night of 6 and 7 April 1916. Launched along the eastern edge of what is now the Newfoundland Memorial, this seventy five man raid led by Leutnants Kaiser, Burger and Sternfeld, was extremely well planned and executed.

The raid, which was prepared and carried out with the utmost attention to detail and determination, hit 2nd Battalion South Wales Borderers, which had only been in the line for three days, extremely hard. This unit was particularly unfortunate, in that all the preparatory registration of mortar and artillery targets had already been completed surreptitiously before they ever entered the line. However, it must be said that this particularly operation was carried out with such skill that the end result would probably have been the same, regardless of who was manning the British positions on that day. A copy of the Operation Plan has survived in the archives in Stuttgart, so it is possible to follow the entire process in detail from start to finish, as this extract makes clear:

A Certificate of Commendation signed by Generalleutnant Stein, commander of XIV Reserve Corps and awarded to Unteroffizier Kaiser of 7th Company RIR 99 on 17 September 1915 for 'excellent performance on patrol'. These certificates were given to encourage men to volunteer for patrols and raids. Participation in a particularly successful operation when the enemy was killed or captured, or if there were seizures of materiel, were always followed by the award of medals or promotion in the field.

Execution of the Operation

On the day of the operation, the patrol groups are to be ready to move in the dugouts of Leiling Mulde (Leiling Hollow) from 8.00 pm. All members of the patrols are to understand that they may not remain in the enemy trenches for longer than fifteen minutes after they leave [the start line] in the sunken road. Commanders of patrols will give the signal to withdraw by means of whistle blasts.

Equipment to be carried by the patrols is to be directed by Oberleutnant Künlen. The commanders are to report to him, on the basis of a personally conducted inspection, that no man is wearing any form of insignia or carrying any written item on his person. The patrols are to wear white armbands on both arms. The leading members of each patrol group are to carry small yellow flags so that they can identify themselves to one another in the event of a clash in the trenches.

Upon return each man is to return to the dugout whence he began the operation. Leutnant Sieber is to prepare a list of those returning and report to the overall commander. Prisoners and captured items are initially to be taken to dugouts I – IV then, as soon as the enemy artillery fire slackens, they are to be brought to the Sector Staff of Beaumont South.

In dugouts V and VI a further rearguard, comprising four sections of the 8th Company under the command of Leutnant Sieber 8th Company, is to be held in readiness. Leutnant Sieber himself will be located in dugout II from 10.00 pm. The companies of the battalion are to be at readiness in their dugouts. They are to remain, with gas masks hung ready for use, at battle readiness until the state of alert is lifted. Sentries in the left half of B5, B6, B7 and B8 are only to be placed in bullet proof observation posts.

Artillery. The artillery is to prepare the break in point A-E for the assault, to neutralise flanking forces from Target Areas 43-46 and 47 Advanced Post, to lay down a barrage behind the break in point and to simulate an attack from B8 to Advanced Post 47 by means of the most powerful and heavy bombardment possible of the Advanced Post 47 and Target Area 48. The sections of trench immediately (up to fifty metres) right and left of the break in point, as well as the third sap to the east of the sunken road are (with the exception of clearance of obstacles) to be bombarded to the same extent as the break in point.

No Man's Land, especially the bank in front of 46 and the sunken road, is to be cleared of possible enemy patrols at the start of

British soldiers captured during the highly successful raid of 6/7 April 1916 being fed at a German field kitchen.

Men of 2nd Battalion South Wales Borderers, captured 6/7 April 1916, being marched through Grévillers into captivity.

the bombardment by the use of shrapnel. In order to deceive the enemy as to the break in point, the fire on neighbouring sectors 43 – 48 is to continue from the beginning of fire preparation until the patrols return and during the outward and inward moves from 10.30 – 10.35 and 10.50 – 11.10 pm, it is to increase to the highest possible intensity. The most probable points for enfilade in Target Areas 45 and 46 are to be engaged with howitzer fire. During the break in of the patrols, the dugouts behind 47 are to be engaged by heavy howitzers, the second and third trenches on Target Areas 47 and 48 are to be fired on with light and heavy howitzers.

Mortars and Earth Mortars. Every available mortar is to be directed against the break in point. At least six medium or heavy mortars are to be employed on the task of shooting three lanes in the enemy obstacle. The four earth mortars in B8 are to bring down the heaviest possible deception fire on Advanced Post 47 from 10.00 – 11.00 pm. Registration of mortars is to occur as long as possible before the operation; at least eight days previously. Mortars and earth mortars are to fire simultaneously and also against neighbouring sectors in order to deceive the enemy. The registration is to be spread over several days, so as not to draw the enemy's attention to the point of assault through unusual mortar fire.

Dress and Equipment. Field caps are to be worn. No shoulderboards or insignia. Identification marks on equipment are to be rendered illegible. No written material in pockets. Belt hooks are to be removed from jackets. As a recognition mark, all participants are to stitch white bands to both right and left arms. Two first field dressings are to be carried in the front jacket pockets. Gas masks are not to be taken. Each man is to carry six hand grenades (four stick grenades on the waist belt), two egg shaped

5. Map of the successful raid of 6/7 April 1916. Visible on the map are the individual routes and break in points of the three groups, as well as the words: Gemeinsamer Weg aller Patrouillen (route common to all raiding parties), Gr.[anat] Loch (Shell Hole), Bereitstell[un]g (final rendezvous), Einschnitt 2,50m tief (cutting 2.50 metres deep) and Pfahl Hindernis (barbed wire obstacle, supported by posts). Back in the Y Ravine area are the location of the overall commander, the Verbandstelle (aid post) and Graben-Rückhalt (4 Gruppen) (four-section, i.e. about thirty six man, reserve).

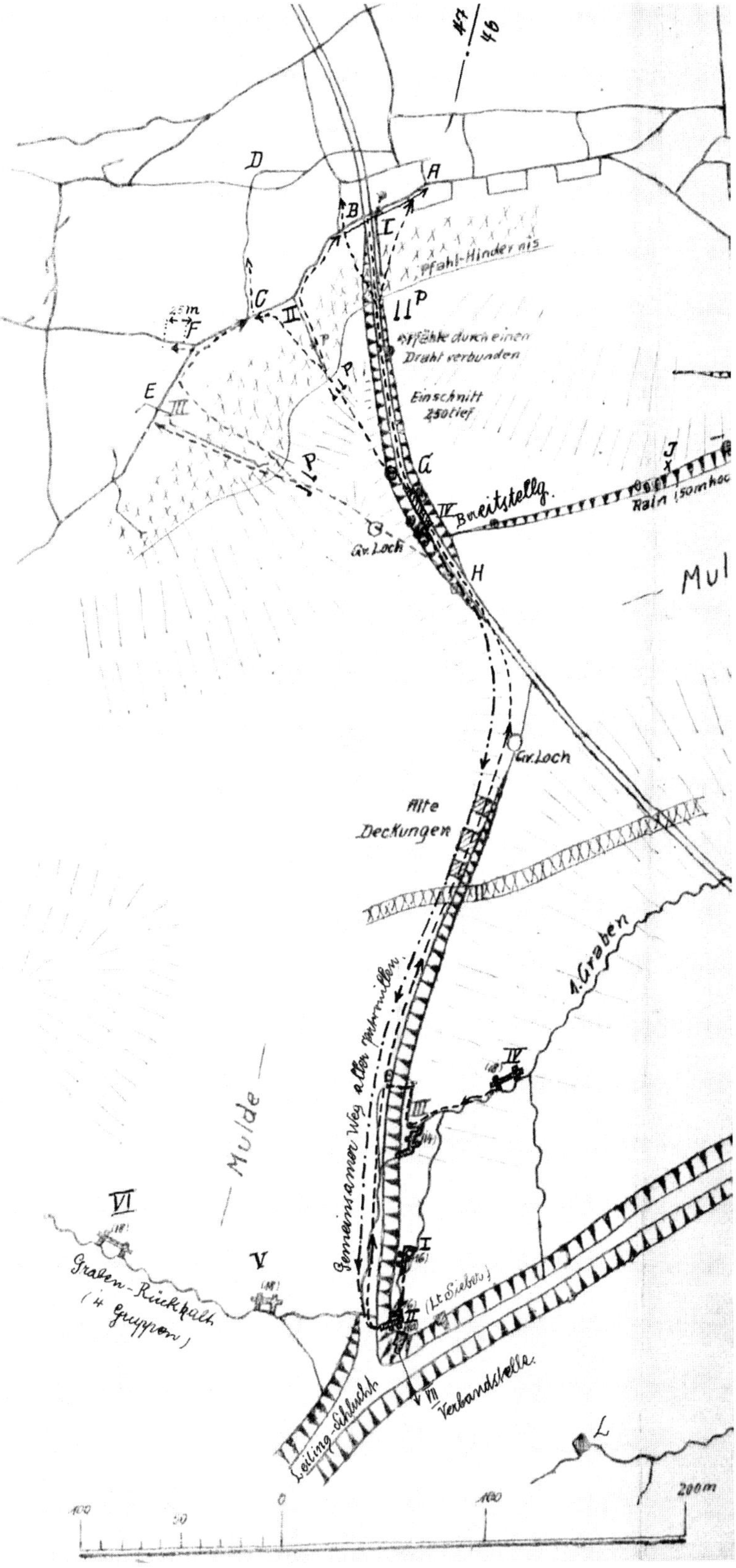

47/46
D
A
B
C
25 m
F
E
Pfahl-Hindernis
Pfähle durch einen Draht verbunden
Einschnitt 2.50 tief
J
Rain 1.50 m hoc
Breitstellg.
Gr. Loch
H
Mul
Gr. Loch
Alte Deckungen
1. Graben
Mulde
Gemeinsamer Weg aller Patrouillen
VI
V
Graben-Rückhalt (4 Gruppen)
(Lt Sieber)
Verbandstelle
Seiling-Schlucht
L
100
50
0
100
200m

grenades in the jacket pockets (tear-off hooks for these on waist belt). Two men of each patrol are to carry rifles, the remainder are to carry pistols, model 08, each with a filled reserve magazine and daggers.(Pistols are to be carried in open holsters and secured round the neck with the strap from a bread pouch).

In addition: four men per patrol wire cutters
              two   ,,   rolled tent halves
              two   ,,   axes
              two   ,,   sharpened trench spades

Commanders of each patrol are to carry small yellow flags, with which to identify themselves in the event of a clash in the trenches. Commanders and NCOs are to have whistles, electric torches and watches with luminous figures. The three commanders are also to carry signalling horns. Commanders are to report the return of their patrols to the commander of the rearguard. The patrols are then to move, as quickly as possibly, the rearguard last, to their departure dugouts, where they are to remain with any prisoners and captured equipment until they receive further orders from the command post.

Prisoners are to be guarded carefully and any documents are to be taken from them immediately. Each man is to give his name to the Control NCO located in the dugout. He in turn is to transmit this immediately to the Control Officer (Dugout II).

The individual officers' patrols and the designated sub-patrols are to make every effort to stick together during the operation. Shouts of 'Hurra!' and all other unnecessary noise are to be avoided during the break in and withdrawal, in order not to betray the break in points. The password is to be given immediately on demand. Possible casualties and their equipment are to be recovered at all costs. Wounded are to be brought in the first instance to the aid post

The divisional commander 26th Reserve Division, Generalleutnant von Soden, presents medals to the members of the raiding party of 6/7 April 1916.

Generalleutnant von Soden visits the front line trenches of RIR 119 after the raid of 6/7 April 1916.

established in dugout VII (Manned by Assistanzarzt Dr. Pietzcker with two medical orderlies and two additional stretcher bearers). As soon as the order has been given by the command post, any wounded and prisoners are to be taken to the rear through the 2nd trench of B6 and Sommergraben to the orderly room of 5th Coy by the churchyard in Beaumont. An advanced dressing station is to be established there under the command of Oberarzt Dr. Kötzle, with two medical orderlies and two stretcher bearers.

Altogether the British 29th Division suffered 112 casualties as a result of this raid: one officer and thirty three other ranks were killed, eight officers and forty two other ranks wounded and twenty-eight other ranks missing (nineteen of whom were captured). The cost to RIR119 was three men killed by a grenade explosion and one man seriously wounded, but successfully evacuated. Smarting from this affront to divisional pride, the British attempted to a launch an ambitious raid of their own on the 30 April, in an attack on the 1st and 10th Companies RIR 119 on Hawthorn Ridge, but the preparations were so blatant and obvious that the defenders monitored the activity then, once the operation was launched, shot the raid to a standstill by means of pre-arranged artillery and small arms fire. In his after action report, Hauptmann von Breuning, the battalion commander, drew attention to all the deficiencies in the preparation and conduct of the operation:

For more than a week the behaviour of the enemy had made it clear that he was planning something against the sector. Almost daily he ranged in his heavy guns against different points. There was a great deal of aerial activity and patrolling ceased. It could not have been a full scale attack, because otherwise more heavy and super-heavy artillery would have been involved. Our patrols also established that he was strengthening his obstacle, so the sole possibility was a trench raid. The only remaining question was, against which sector was it planned?...The ground most favours an assault against the right hand Zange (Pincer = Hawthorn Redoubt). There are covered approaches and it is not enfiladed from anywhere. It only presents a narrow front and cannot expect fire support from the flanks. On the evening of [27 April], the sector commander informed the commander of Artillery Group A that the right hand Zange was in special danger and an increased state of alert was maintained throughout the night... On the 28 April it was striking that there was heavy fire against the left flank and a great deal of shrapnel fire on the obstacle, which was somewhat damaged. It was repaired and the attack did not occur... A daylight

Damage caused to the German trenches on Hawthorn Ridge during the abortive raid of 30 April 1916.

British arms and equipment seized after the failed raid of 30 April 1916.

Major Schäfer, commanding officer 3rd Battalion RIR 119, together with two noted patrol leaders from his battalion.

patrol on 29 April discovered and recovered two short arrows, surmounted by shiny bottles in front of the 1st Company, which they discovered pointed the way to a small hollow in the ground, which offered a covered approach... For the night 29- 30 April, there was once again an increased state of alert, then the tip of the wood was very noticeably hit with 240 millimetre shells and heavy mortars... After it went dark, all was quiet, but at 12.30 am there was suddenly extremely heavy artillery and mortar fire and at the same time machine gun fire... Two of our patrols went forward immediately... to meet the enemy in No Man's Land if possible... Red flares called for immediate defensive fire from our artillery... [and] the patrols later confirmed that it came down exactly as intended.

For the next sixty minutes all sub-sector commanders and observers within range reported the origin and intensity of the incoming fire, so that the artillery group commander could switch his guns between fire missions and engage new targets with his stand by batteries as required. At around 1.30 am, the artillery was ordered to reduce the rate of fire dramatically, but to be ready to re-engage if an enemy assault did in fact occur. Simultaneously all the companies in the sector launched additional patrols forward. By 2.00 am, the patrols were back in; those that had spent the entire time forward, reporting that the British had indeed tried for some time to launch the raid, but that they could not get forward through the defensive barrage.

Just as the raid of 6/7 April had been a model of its kind, the conduct of the defence on 30 April was outstanding. Communications and coordination of the defensive battle, right down to platoon level had been first class. Despite the expenditure by the British army of 4,000 – 5,000 artillery shells and mortar bombs, casualties amongst the defenders had been negligible and the damage to the trenches was

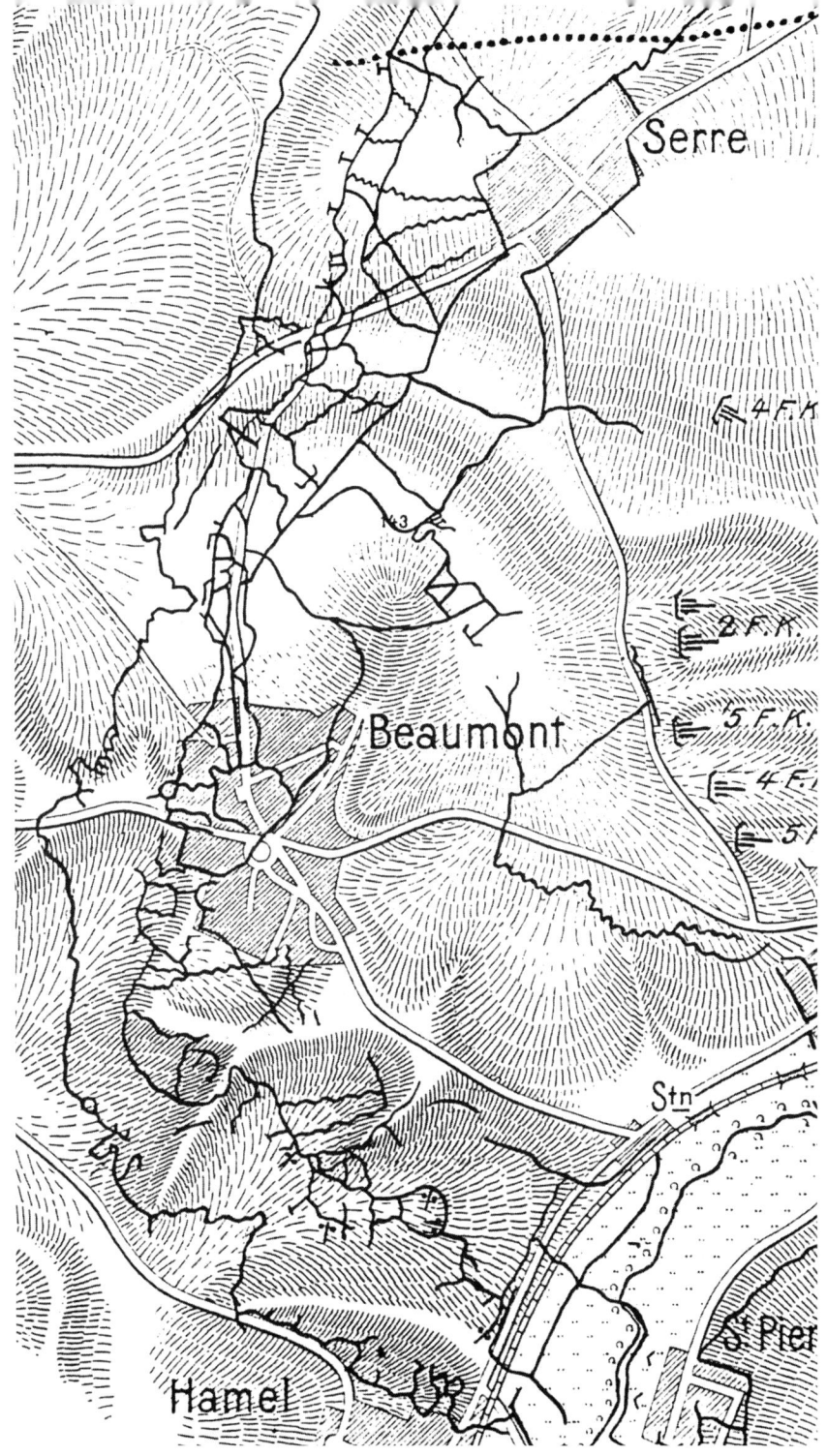

6. The embryonic trench network in the Beaumont Hamel area in early 1915. Only the front line trace of the opposing lines is shown.

quickly repaired. The British casualties, together with quantities of captured equipment, were recovered from No Man's Land; the dead being buried in a plot of the divisional cemetery in Miraumont. Lance Corporal Fry and Privates Lloyd and Tordoff still lie in a CWGC extension to the civilian cemetery in Miraumont.

Naturally the British army also mounted successful raids from time to time; the Germans coming to terms with the fact that if an operation was well planned and sufficient mortar and artillery fire was brought to bear, it was almost impossible to prevent determined raiders from forcing their way into the forward trenches. One such occasion occurred in the early hours of 4 June 1916, when three officers and 48 other ranks of 1st Battalion Lancashire Fusiliers gained entry into the forward trench of Sector B1 (Hawthorn Ridge), which at the time was held by 8th Company RIR 119. Reports written subsequently by attackers and attacked are largely in agreement with each other, but differ in detail and emphasis. After a short, sharp bombardment involving the use of some 8,000 rounds, the raid went in. The British report speaks of cutting the wire at one point with a Bangalore torpedo (a length of pipe packed with explosive); the German one that an intact torpedo nine metres long was recovered after the raid – possible this was an unused spare. The British claim to have searched a 100 metre section of trench, 'which was found to be vacated by the Germans', carrying off notice boards and papers. The German report makes no mention of this, but does state that some men were wounded by grenades thrown from the wire obstacle and others by grenades thrown down into a dugout.

Possibly each side was trying to put the best gloss on events. What is certain is that the British received a poor return from an operation which had taken a lot of effort to mount and they had even less success as the date of the major summer offensive approached. In the closing days of June 1916, there were several completely abortive attempts between the Serre-Mailly road and the river Ancre to conduct raids on the forward positions, in an attempt to judge the efficacy of the bombardment. Each was driven off with heavy losses in dead, wounded and captured and one man from the Royal Fusiliers, Private Josef Lipmann, deserting from a patrol on 28 June, provided the German defenders with a great deal of information about the forthcoming attack. It was an indifferent, but not altogether surprising, end to a period when the German regiments had generally had the upper hand.

Chapter 4

THE BATTLE OF SERRE JUNE 1915

D ESPITE THE CONSTANT MINOR OPERATIONS of active trench warfare, the late winter and spring of 1915 was a quiet period in the Beaumont Hamel area. One result was that when the spring battles around Notre Dame de Lorette and Vimy were raging north of Arras, a reorganisation of the front of the 26th Reserve Division permitted 2nd, 3rd and 4th Battalions RIR 99 to be withdrawn and sent north as reinforcements. Their sector was taken over by RIR 119 and 1st Bn RIR 99 stayed behind in Miraumont as sector reserve. The three battalions were to be badly missed when, in mid-June 1915, the French army launched a determined assault on a bulge in the line to the west of Serre. It is entirely possible that this was designed to divert German resources away from Vimy. Locally it could be justified easily by the fact that possession of the heights around Serre was the key to any potential advance on Bapaume and Cambrai. Despite the fact that the main weight of the French assaults went in slightly to the north of its sector of responsibility, it certainly presented 26th Reserve Division with its biggest challenge since the battles of the previous December.

The preparations for the attack were quite drawn out. Already by the end of May the defenders had noted an increase in aerial activity, artillery being ranged in, extensive troop movements, saps and communication trenches being pushed forward and changes in patrol activity to its front. There was time to task air reconnaissance flights and to put in place the necessary counter-actions or, rather, what were deemed to be adequate measures; the devastating effect of concentrated heavy artillery fire on the trenches was underestimated by the German defenders at the time. The existence of two particularly significant communication trenches opposite the southern sector of the 52nd Infantry Division, which was directly responsible for the Serre sector, was confirmed by aerial photography on 5 June 1915. This was sufficient proof for XIV Reserve Corps to issue an appreciation stating that an attack against 52nd Division was probably imminent and that the sector of 26th Reserve Division north of the Ancre could be involved as well.

Immediate steps were taken to regroup the artillery to meet this assessed threat and to call for reinforcing batteries to be sent forward. Infantry reserves were identified and placed where they would be able to react swiftly, so by 6th June 1915 the divisional reserves north of the Ancre were grouped as follows:

1st Battalion RIR 99, commanded by Major Freiherr Gerhard von Meerscheidt-Hüllessem in Miraumont, with one company forward on Hill 143, northeast of Beaumont Hamel. This is the modern point 138, which was later developed into *Feste Soden* (Soden Redoubt).

¹/₂ 2nd Battalion RIR 121 (7th and 8th Companies) commanded by Hauptmann Guido Nagel (Who later gave his name to *Nagelgraben*, an important trench on Redan Ridge), also located at Miraumont.

1st Battalion IR 180 at Miraumont under divisional command. (3rd Battalion IR 180, commanded by Major Scupin, also in the same area, was designated Corps reserve).

All the troops in and around Miraumont were located close to divisional headquarters, so it was a straightforward matter to pass orders to them. 5th and 6th Companies RIR 121, located in Courcelette, were the only reserves south of the Ancre at the time.

Additional measures taken were the establishment of an additional ammunition dump at Irles and all means of communications forward and to the flanks were checked and tested thoroughly. Up until this point links with 52nd Infantry Division had been tenuous. Urgent steps were taken to improve matters and exact chains of command and liaison arrangements were further refined. Two batteries of 3rd Battalion RFAR 26 were moved from Pozières to the area around the Ruined Mill and orders for relief gun crews and the supply of replacement guns were issued. All was ready, but the anticipated attack did not materialise. French artillery and heavy mortar fire continued to be brought down on the Toutvent Farm – Beaumont Hamel sector. The trenches and dugouts suffered badly and telephone links were destroyed. By 3.00 am 7 June 1915, 52nd Division was reporting, 'Trenches flattened. Expect attack tomorrow. Request artillery support'.

There was feverish activity within 26th Reserve Division. Fresh orders were sent to the artillery and the reserves were moved into new locations as follows:

3rd Battalion IR 180 from Miraumont to the valley to the east of Puisieux and placed at the disposal of 52nd Infantry Division.

1st Battalion RIR 99 to Hill 143 northeast of Beaumont Hamel

¹/₂ 2nd Battalion RIR 121 (7th and 8th Companies) from Miraumont to the Artillery Hollow east of Point 143.

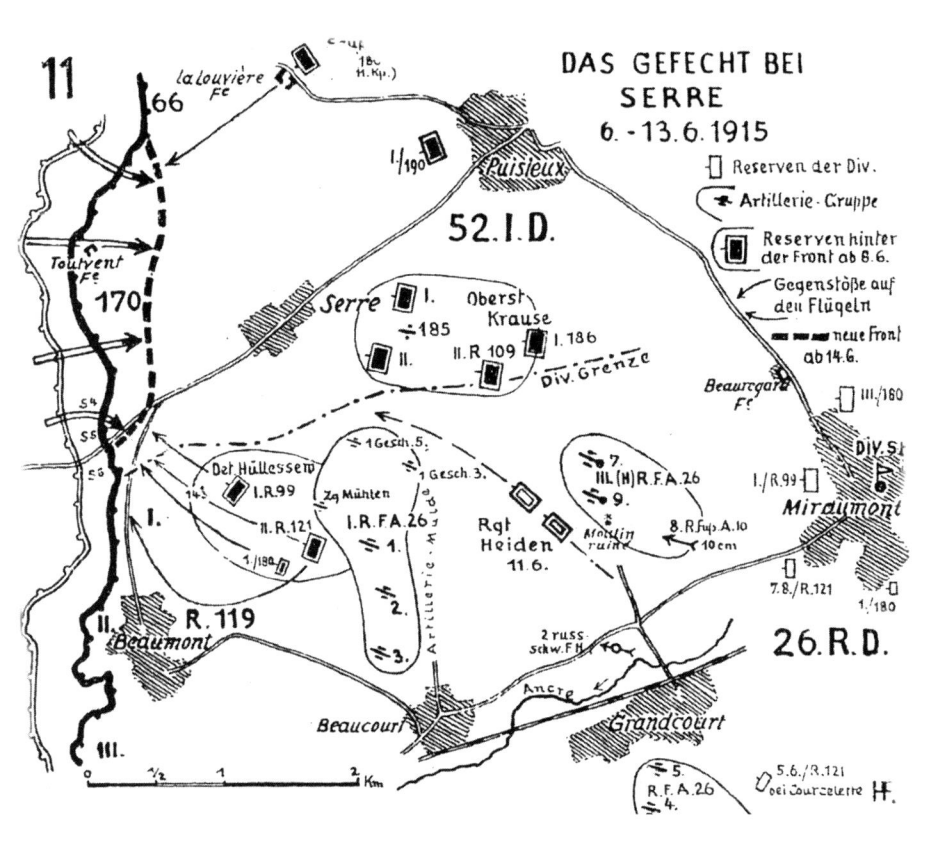

7. Location and moves of artillery units and infantry reserves during the Battle of Serre June 1915. The key states that the arrows relate to 'counter-attacks on the flanks'.

1/2 2nd Battalion RIR 121 (5th and 6th Companies) from Courcelette to Grandcourt.

The two howitzer batteries of 26th Reserve Division and the heavy guns of 8th Battery Reserve Foot Artillery Regiment 10 were directed to superimpose their fire onto flanking targets to the north which were being engaged by the artillery of 52nd Infantry Division. Having done everything possible, the staff of divisional headquarters could only wait anxiously for news. About 11.30 am the first reports arrived. The French army had succeeded in breaking in around Toutvent Farm and capturing it. The attack had then swept forward on the flanks of Serre, but had been held in heavy close-quarter fighting. So far, though threatened, the sector held by IR 170 just to the north of Redan Ridge was holding.

XIV Reserve Corps had not been idle during this period, feeding reserves forward to Miraumont and Beauregard Farm. From the Corps reserve came 2nd Battalion RIR 109 and 3rd Battalion RIR 111 from

28th Reserve Division, whilst Second Army released 1st and 2nd Battalions IR 185, together with their machine gun company, 1st Battalion IR 186 and 1st Battalion IR 190 from Infantry Brigade 185, together with the brigade engineer company. As a first step, 3rd Bn IR 180 was moved to La Louvière Farm, under command of the 52nd Infantry Division. It had been hoped to launch a counter-attack that same night, but this turned out to be over ambitious. In the generally confused situation it proved to be completely impossible to distribute orders and move the reserves to the necessary locations.

Of more immediate concern to 26th Reserve Division was the situation on Redan Ridge, especially the northern sector forward of Hill 143 in the area between where Serre Road Number 2 Cemetery and the French memorial chapel stand today. This was held by 1st Battalion RIR 119, commanded by Hauptmann Breuning, who was able, with considerable difficulty, to report that, although the sub-sector was under constant heavy fire, he had not thus far come under direct attack. His men were succeeding in making rough and ready repairs to the position itself, but all his telephone links were destroyed and, more importantly, he had no contact with IR 170 on his right. His flank was in the air. Because junctions between formations are weak points in the defence at the best of times, Generalleutnant von Soden ordered 5th and 6th Companies RIR 121 forward during the evening of 7 June to link up with the other forward companies of 2nd Battalion, which provided him with a complete battalion back in dead ground ready to undertake any necessary counter-action under its commander Hauptmann Nagel.

By the morning of 8 June, the defenders had assembled reserves to the north, east and south of Serre. To the east of the village, Oberst Krause had command of 1st and 2nd Battalions IR 185, together with 2nd Battalion RIR 109 and could also call on 1st Battalion IR 190 in Puisieux if the French succeeded in entering Serre. From 26th Reserve Division, Major von Meerscheidt-Hüllessem, located behind Hill 143, now had 1st Battalion RIR 99 and 2nd Battalion RIR 121 at his disposal to prevent any breakthrough between Serre and Beaumont Hamel. Meanwhile the pressure on 1st Battalion RIR 119 continued to grow and casualties increased until, on 9 June, 8th Company RIR 121, 1st Company IR 180 and later 6th Company RIR 121, together with elements of 1st Battalion RIR 99 had to be fed into the battle on its right flank, where a concerted effort was made by means of a hand grenade attack to re-establish contact with 1st Bn IR 170 under Hauptmann Guflmann. That same day 3rd Battalion IR 180, counter-

La Louvière Farm, damaged during the Battle of Serre.

attacking against La Louvière Farm, gained ground and captured some 100 prisoners, who revealed that the attack had been launched by 21st French Division of XI Corps, together with a brigade from XIV Corps and heavy artillery from Castelnau's Second Army.

On 10 June there was a further serious French attempt to attack the junction between IR 170 and RIR 119. The remnants of IR 170 held on doggedly through a heavy one hour artillery bombardment. This was followed up by an infantry assault about 5.00 pm which, thanks to the assistance of 1st Company IR 180 and 8th Company RIR 121, was beaten off with heavy French casualties. Nevertheless French gains meant that there was a risk that these companies, which had also suffered severely, would be encircled. This was avoided by means of a controlled withdrawal by sections behind Hill 143, but this meant that once again the right flank of RIR 119 was hanging in the air. Fortunately the commander of RIR 119 had been alive to the possibility and had moved the remaining 5th and 6th Companies RIR 121from the Hill 143 concentration area to the right flank of his regiment, using a circuitous but covered route via Beaumont Hamel.

Front line trenches along the Serre- Mailly road, hastily constructed at the end of the Battle of Serre.

Hauptmann Nagel's men occupied the original second trench, filling in to the left of 7th Company forward near the Serre – Mailly road.

IR 170, which had been bearing the brunt of the attacks, was in a very weakened state so, from 10 June, 26th Reserve Division was given responsibility for the entire Serre sector. An intended attack by Major von Meerscheidt-Hüllessem's men to relieve pressure on the RIR 119

Front line positions being repaired after the Battle of Serre.

right flank was never launched, due to numerous insurmountable difficulties, but help was at hand. I Bavarian Corps had pulled together from various sources a two-battalion regiment under a Major Heiden. Generaleutnant von Wundt was given command of this regiment and four other reserve battalions and was ordered to throw the French back out of the southern S6 sector (just to the north of RIR 119) and to take back the high ground to the west of Serre. This attack, launched with determination during the night 11/12 June, was only partially successful. One battalion did succeed in digging in on the high ground. S6 was firmly in German hands, but Heiden's men could make no progress. The Corps Commander XIV Reserve Corps forbade a resumption of the attack on 12 June in order to avoid further casualties.

It was decided instead to seal off the French gains by means of the

Major von Meerscheidt-Hüllessem, who put in another strong personal performance during the Battle of Serre, photographed in the newly-constructed Heidenkopf.

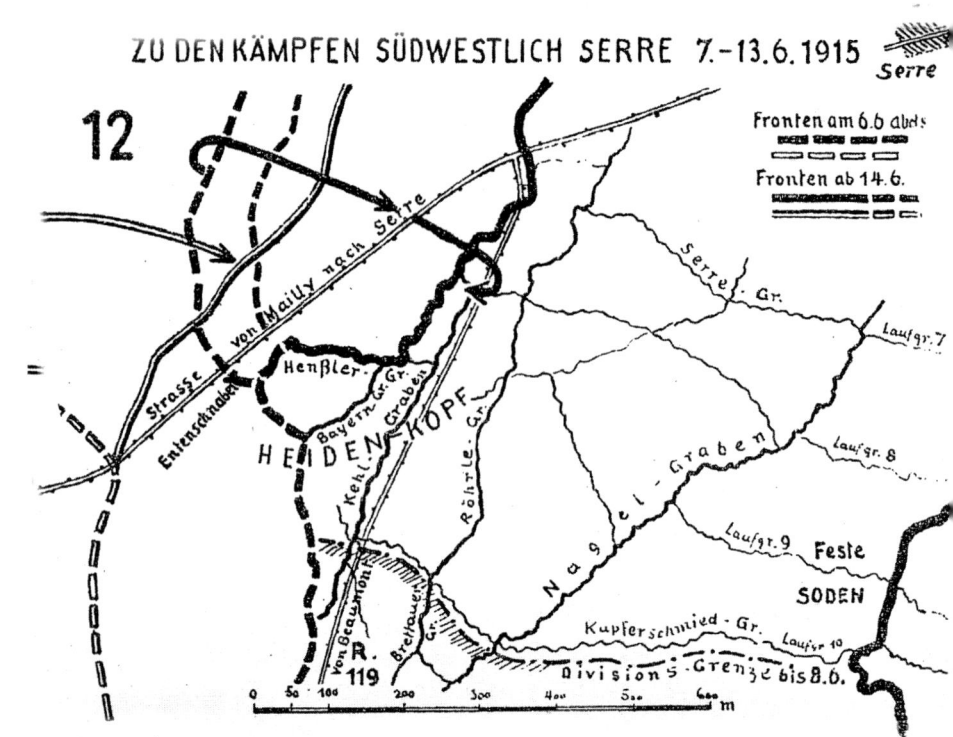

8. Ground gained and lost during the Battle of Serre. Of note is the speed with which the Heidenkopf and associated trenches were dug.

construction of a new trench system and work began immediately on a new line to link Serre with the road junction opposite what is now Serre Road Number 1 Cemetery. Whilst this work was still underway, the French army launched one last attempt on 13 June to breakthrough on the inter-divisional boundary in this area. There were slight gains north of the Serre-Mailly road, but to the south the defence, though under intense pressure, held firm and threw back the attack with severe casualties. Hauptmann Nagel, commanding officer of 2nd Battalion RIR 121, who had been a tower of strength during these tense days, was killed during this final attack, as was Hauptmann Hornberger, whilst in command of 5th Company RIR 121. Hauptmann von Raben of 7th Company RIR 121 assumed command of the battalion and the sector. Use was made of the manpower of the reinforcing units in the area to dig the Heidenkopf and improve communication trenches to the rear area, especially towards Hill 143.

13 June saw the end of French infantry attacks, although there continued to be artillery exchanges for some time to come. Naturally at

the time it was impossible to say if the French intended to resume offensive operations, so digging went ahead feverishly under the command of Major Heiden at the northern end of Redan Ridge and Oberstleutnant Krause further north towards Serre. By 18 June, Heiden's Bavarians had been released back to their own formation and RIR 119 had assumed command of the entire area around where the fighting had been raging in this locality. By the end of June the monotony of trench warfare had replaced the intensity of the recent fighting and it was time to take stock. The German army decided that the Battle of Serre had not been intended as a serous attempt at a breakthrough; rather more it was launched as a diversion of German effort away from the fighting to the north of Arras and to improve their positions locally. If that was the case, the fact that the battle ended with the German defenders still in possession of the high ground

Men of IR 180 in the Entenschnabel (Duck's Bill), separated from the French by only a three metre barrier. See Map 9 for location.

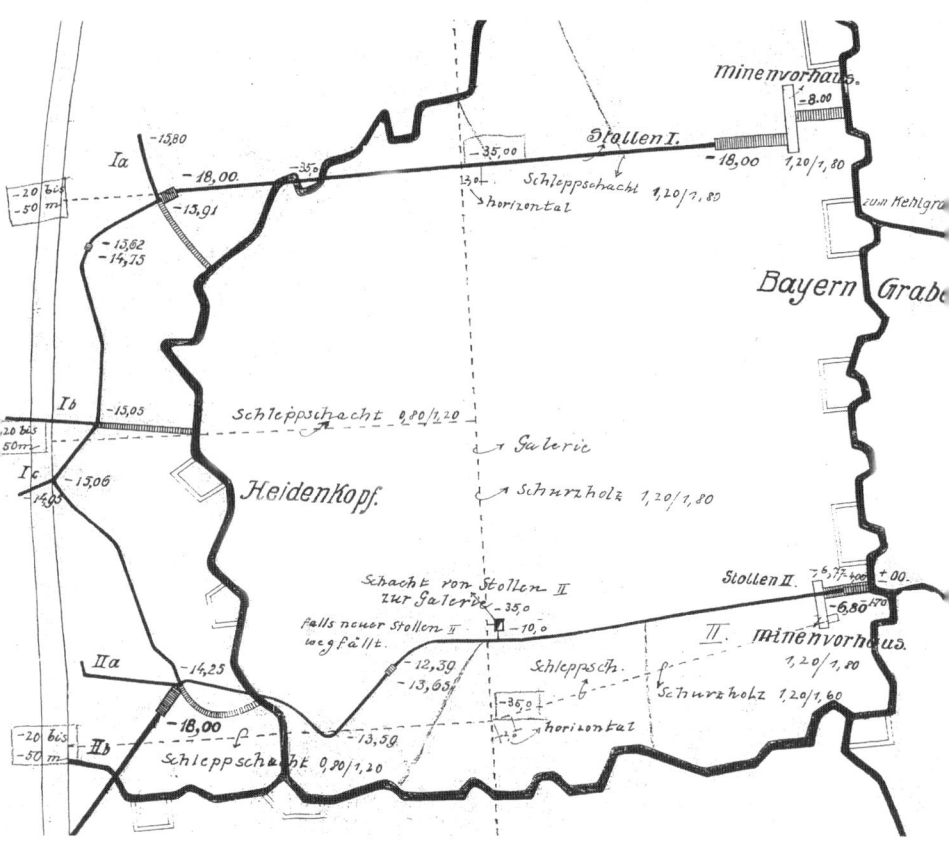

9. Diagram of mining activities beneath the Heidenkopf as at spring 1916. These galleries were the basis for the four German mines blown here on 1 July 1916.

around Serre, whilst the French were condemned to positions in the low ground to the west and the fact that the attack had been held from within the resources of XIV Reserve Corps suggests that it was not particularly successful.

Nevertheless it would be wrong to dismiss this battle as a mere footnote to the history of the area. To begin with the German generals were very concerned that, despite prior warning and having had time to take counter-measures, the front line of 52nd Infantry Division had been broken on a two and a half kilometre front by a combination of heavy artillery and mortar fire and a determined infantry attack. In addition, despite strenuous counter-attacking efforts, it had not proved possible to achieve the psychologically valuable aim of restoring the original line. The German chain of command sat down after the fighting had died away and did some hard thinking and detailed analysis about what had gone well and what had gone badly during the

Battle of Serre. Generalleutnant Freiherr von Soden later described it as, 'an extremely instructive preparation for the Battle of the Somme, during which lessons learned at Serre were of the highest value'. It was not just at divisional level and below that lessons were learned. Within only two weeks of the end of the fighting around Serre, reports had gone up the chain of command to Second Army Headquarters and the Army Commander, General von Below himself, had released an important operational instruction, which had profound consequences for the way the defensive positions were developed during the remaining year before the main battle:

Deep dugouts, proof against even direct hits by heavy artillery, which are now available almost everywhere, carry with them a danger that cannot be treated lightly. They make the swift occupation of the firing step, in the event of a surprise attack, more difficult. This was highlighted during the recent battles near Hébuterne. There can be no doubt that the French army succeeded in several places in breaking into our position, almost without being engaged, whilst some of our troops were still sheltering in the dugouts, where they were then taken prisoner.

In order to prevent this, the entrances to dugouts are to be widened and they are to be equipped with two entrances. The desire to dig unnecessarily deep is also to be discouraged. A depth of three metres is sufficient to provide protection from a direct hit of up to 155 millimetre calibre.

The main point, however, is to make certain that the men in the dugouts are warned of an enemy attack in sufficient time and that they then exit the dugouts as quickly as possible. A wide variety of means may be employed in order to raise the alarm: bells, drums, voice tubes, shouting down etc. To ensure that the procedure will work when it is needed, the alarm system must be exercised. In the same way, the men must be drilled intensively, to pour out of the dugouts swiftly and to race to their positions. The regiments are to lay down the necessary words of command for this procedure.

One essential pre-requisite, in order to remove any doubt about the matter, is to establish who is in charge of each dugout, so that, if in the event of an enemy attack, certain groups do not man their battle positions in time, the relevant commander can be court-martialled. I require the necessary action to be taken with the utmost urgency.

For its part 26th Reserve Division, realising that although through the skill of its gunners and the courage of its infantrymen it had been

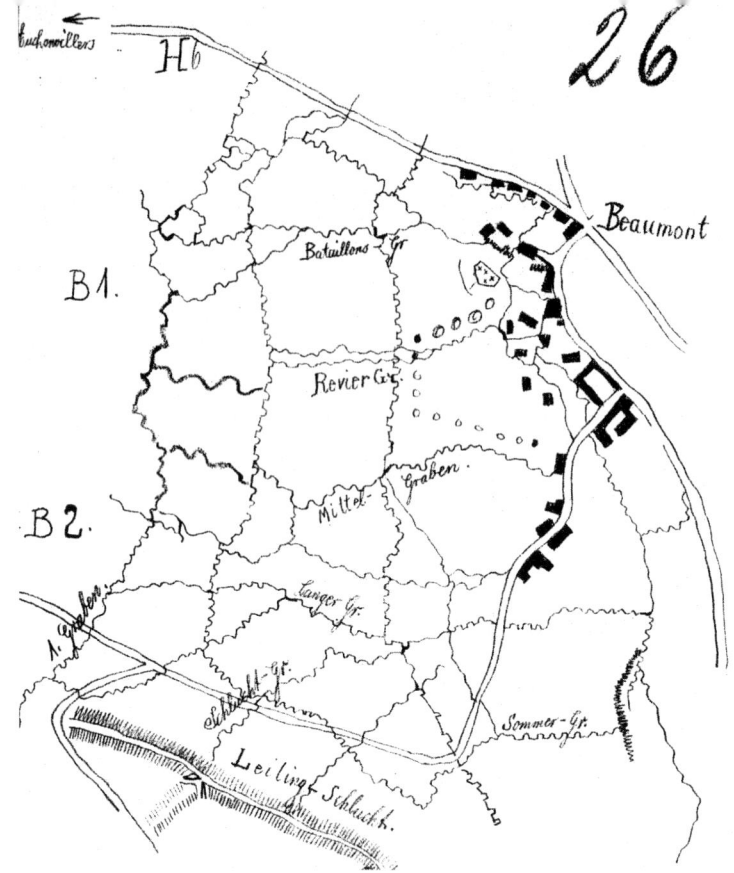

10. *The trench layout south of Beaumont Hamel on 8 June 1916. Compare the sectors with those on Map 1 on page 12, which were so designated after XIV Reserve Corps had inserted additional formations into the front line.*

possible to seal off the French attack and to prevent it from being expanded horizontally or in depth, the battle had, in fact, been a close run thing locally. All ranks applied themselves assiduously to the improvement of their positions and operational procedures. The value of the ground behind Hill 143 had been underlined to such an extent that a new field fortification, *Feste Soden* (Soden Redoubt), was constructed there; it was to play a crucial role in the 1916 fighting. Elsewhere nearby the *Grallsburg* and *Feste Alt-Württemberg* (Beaucourt Redoubt) were further developed, as were numerous key locations south of the Ancre. The Battle of Serre had cost it seven officers killed and 900 other dead and wounded, but by 1 July 1916, having applied what it had learned at so high a price, it presented a formidable defensive front to the British army, utterly smashing the combined efforts of VIII and X Corps at an appalling cost to the attackers.

Chapter 5

THE BOMBARDMENT AND 1 JULY 1916

AS A RESULT OF UNMISTAKEABLE SIGNS, observed from spring 1916 onwards, that a huge Allied attack was looming, the German Second Army regrouped its forces so as best to meet the threat. The pitifully few reserves which could be spared were incorporated into the defences, so it was possible to reduce the width of company frontages to some extent and to ensure that troops were available to man the entire depth of the Forward and, in addition, the Intermediate and Second Positions. The defensive main effort was to be north of the Somme initially, so in order to improve force ratios in the area deemed to be most at risk, the 10th Bavarian Reserve Division, located south of the River Somme, was broken up and its three Regiments – 6th and 8th Reserve and 16th – were moved north individually in reinforcing roles. Although one of these regiments, namely 8th Reserve, was allocated to 26th Reserve Division, because of the importance of the Thiepval Ridge it was deployed south of the Ancre; the defence of Beaumont Hamel, therefore, depended entirely on the efforts of the two regiments of 51 Reserve Brigade, a situation which remained unchanged for many weeks, until the entire Division was withdrawn for rest and reconstitution on 10 October 1916 and even after that RIR 121 returned to play a role in the final battles on Redan Ridge.

By the end of June 1916, the relevant headquarters were deployed as follows: 26th Reserve Division: Biefvillers, Artillery Commander: Grévillers, 51 Reserve Brigade, commanded by Generalleutnant von Wundt, in the *Alte-Garde Stellung* (Old Guards Position), RIR 119 *Grallsburg* and RIR 121 Feste *Alt-Württemberg* (Beaucourt Redoubt). RIR

Generalleutnant von Wundt, commander 51 Reserve Brigade.

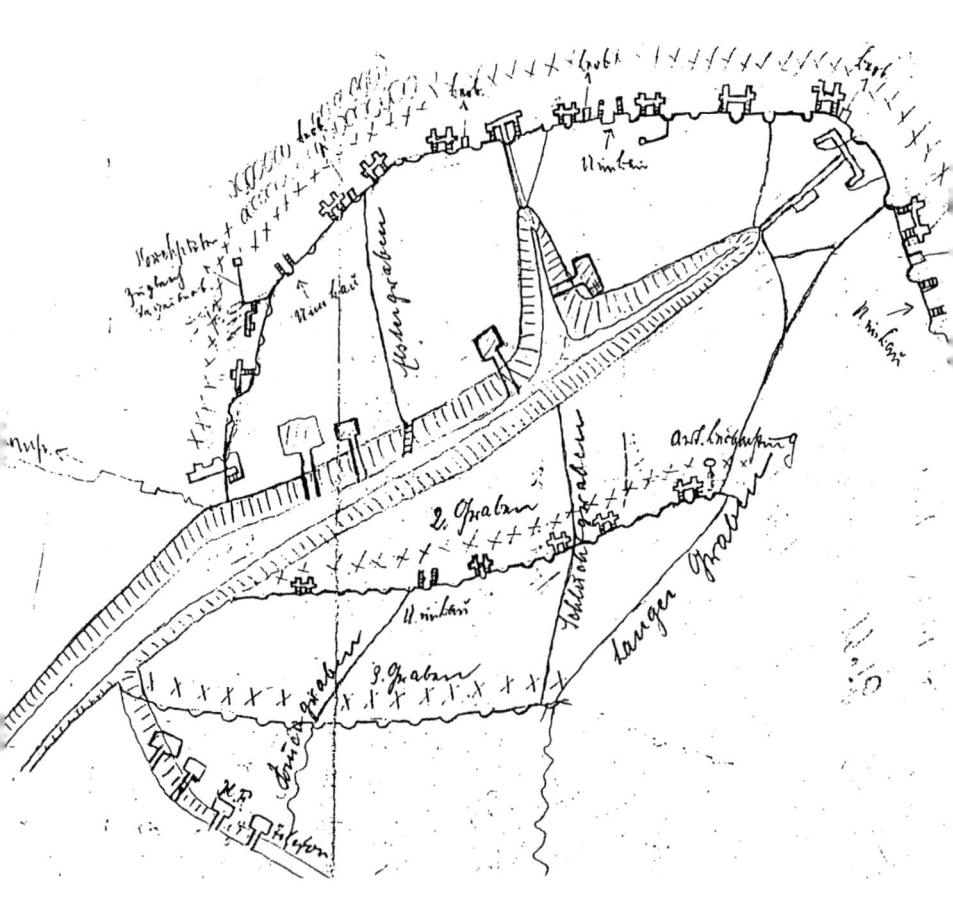

11. *Sketch of the underground workings in and around Y Ravine in June 1916. Note the dugout marked 'K.F'. (Kompanie Fuhrer = company commander) at the bottom of the sketch.*

119 was responsible for the sector from Beaumont Hamel to the Ancre, with the units of RIR 121 defending Redan Ridge right up to the Serre-Mailly road. The first three weeks of June had seen ceaseless activity by the men of the brigade as they sought to improve their positions and increase their stockpiles of ammunition. Both the first and second trenches of the First Position were fully garrisoned and, in places, men were found to occupy the third line trenches as well. The battalions which were theoretically at rest were brought forward into the intermediate position between *Feste Soden* (Soden Redoubt) and the *Grallsburg*.

Everything that could be dug in or placed underground, from spare

Oberstleutnant von Ziegesar, commander RIR 119, outside his command post on the Grallsburg.

ammunition to entire field kitchens, disappeared downwards. The morning of 24 June dawned bright and sunny on the Somme. Throughout the 51 Reserve Brigade area the men had breakfasted and were about to continue with the digging and mining that had characterised daily routine for many months past when suddenly, at 6.30 am, the Allied bombardment opened along the forward positions with a deafening series of explosions. Countless shrapnel rounds burst above the trenches, sending dense showers of the half-ounce lead balls whistling down through the trees and onto the half-ruined roofs of Beaumont Hamel. Much the same style of bombardment continued throughout the first day, with the *Heidenkopf* (Quadrilateral) coming in for particular punishment. The defenders could not see the point of all this shrapnel fire, which damaged neither the trenches nor the men who were sheltering in their dugouts throughout the day. The command post of RIR 121 in *Feste Alt-Württemberg* received a direct

Oberstleutnant Josenhans, commander RIR 121, contemplates his badly damaged command post in Feste Alt-Württemberg, July 1916. Josenhans died in 1919 as a result of the exhaustion and nervous strain of commanding a regiment throughout the war.

Feind greift an (*Sperrfeuer*)

2 Rote Sterne

Vernichtungsfeuer
(nur auf Befehl der Komp. Führer oder ihrer Vorgesetzten)

2 Grüne Sterne

Feuer vorverlegen
(nur in ruhigen Kampflagen anwenden)

2 gelbe schwebende Kugeln

Flare signal codes for the opening of the Battle of the Somme July 1916. From the top, two red stars = enemy attacking, fire artillery defensive fire; two green stars = bring down destructive fire. This message was generally restricted to company commanders and above; two yellow parachute flares, = lengthen the range. Of these signals, the first was by far the most important and most frequently used.

hit, but luckily it had overhead cover made from reinforced concrete so, although the occupants were shaken and the roof was damaged, it was possible to go on exercising command from there.

Towards evening the bombardment slackened, but just as it seemed that it would be possible to organise forward re-supply, the shells crashed down once more, producing a wall of exploding shells and preventing any movement along the approach routes between Grandcourt, Beaucourt or Beaucourt Station and the forward positions. There was nothing for it but for the ration parties to withdraw. It was much the same story in and around Beaumont Hamel on 25 June but, as the day wore on, more and heavier high explosive shell began to be mixed with the shrapnel rounds and the sector seemed to have been chosen to receive particularly close attention from aerial observers. British aircraft circled constantly, trying to locate dugout entrances and no fewer than eighteen balloons were up directing artillery fire. RIR

121 continued to adjust the placement of its sub units, moving its 3rd Battalion forward to the Intermediate Position and its 1st Battalion forward into Nagel Graben. Unfortunately, hardly had the battalion arrived in position than the commanding officer, Hauptmann Freiherr von Ziegesar, was mortally wounded. He died the following day. His death was a body blow to the entire regiment. He was one of the original officers who had marched off to war in 1914 in command of 11th Company and had proved himself repeatedly during the next two years. That night RIR 119 called forward the remaining companies of its 2nd Battalion, which had been held back in Miraumont and deployed them in depth along the rear trenches of the dense web which constituted the defences of the village and its surrounding area. Miraumont itself was under heavy fire, one heavy round hitting the church and wrecking the roof completely. Even at this late stage there were still some civilians living in Miraumont. This latest shelling drove them out and they fled, leaving a pathetic trail of personal possessions marking their route to the safety of the rear area.

There was a new development on 26 June. The artillery fire was

Hauptmann Maul of RIR 119, who was killed in action on 6 September 1916.

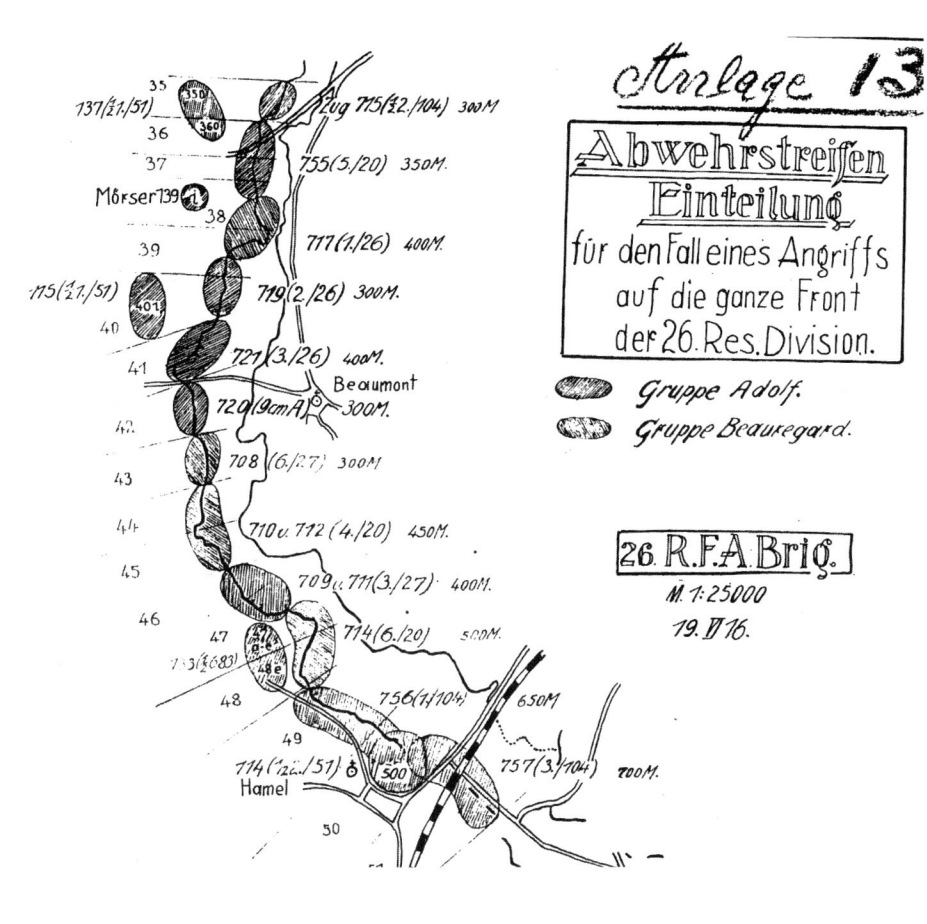

12. The defensive artillery fire plan for 51 Reserve Brigade, dated 19 June 1916. As well as listing the enemy target areas (35 to 50), the area covered by artillery or mortar defensive fire zones is shown. The responsibility for each is split between Artillery Group Adolf and Beauregard and the sub-unit (battery) responsible for each is laid down; e.g. 5./20 = 5th Battery, 2nd Battalion, Field Artillery Regiment 20, 3./104 = 3rd Battery, 1st Battalion, Field Artillery Regiment 104. These two groups were commanded by Oberst Erlenbusch, commander of RFAR 26.

lifted about midday and no fewer than nine cloud gas releases took place in successive waves against Beaumont North. It was impossible to say if the clouds of gas were designed to cover an attack, so it was necessary on every occasion to man the trenches as a precautionary measure. Between each release there was a further conventional bombardment, the idea being to catch the defenders in the open before they had a chance to regain their dugouts. This tactic caused some casualties and there were many close shaves. An attempt to subject

Beaumont South to the same treatment between 3.00 pm and 4.00 pm was a complete failure; the gas drifted northeastwards into the Ancre Valley, missing the German lines entirely. Massively heavy shells were used against Hawthorn Ridge that day and the nerves of the men of 9th Company RIR 119 suffered correspondingly. These so-called 'aerial torpedoes', actually large calibre delayed-action shells, hammered down on the positions north and south of the Beaumont – Auchonvillers road in particular. They left craters up to three metres deep and four – five metres wide and there was great concern that even the deepest dugouts might not be proof against these explosions. Extraordinary to relate there were no fatal casualties as a result of this fire, but some men had to be evacuated severely shocked.

After three days of bombardment, the British army pushed forward patrols to assess the effectiveness of the fire. One such, during the early hours of 27 June, closed to within grenade throwing range of 9th Company RIR 119 on Hawthorn Ridge, but thanks to a combination of prompt work by Reserve Leutnant Breitmeier, who was duty officer, and the alertness of the sentries, the attempt was detected and driven off by a combination of small arms and artillery fire. Throughout 28 June Beaumont Hamel was kept under extremely heavy fire and was subject to repeated gas attacks. The *Heidenkopf* was hit so hard by heavy mortars and artillery rounds that the decision was taken to evacuate it. For the first time the giant 380 mm shells were fired at the village and the *Leiling Stollen* (Leiling Mined Dugout, which was situated on a reverse slope in Sector B4, about six hundred metres south of the church in Beaumont Hamel) was subject to constant fire from 230 mm howitzers throughout the day. This fire was directed from the air and its entrances were collapsed. This was a common occurrence by this stage of the bombardment, forcing the defenders to take considerable risks in the open to dig them out once more. There was also a determined trench raid launched by the British 29th Division against both ends of the *Leiling Schlucht* (Y Ravine) prior to dawn that day, but it was driven off with heavy losses by 2nd, 10th and 11th Coys RIR 119. A patrol sent forward in the immediate aftermath of this raid captured several prisoners, whose interrogations yielded useful information.

The bombardment ground on. Sometimes there were further attempts at gas attacks, but none enjoyed any success. There were other raids all along the brigade front from Redan Ridge to the heights above the Ancre in the early hours of 29 and 30 June, but all were beaten back without any difficulty. Nevertheless the incessant fire had had a

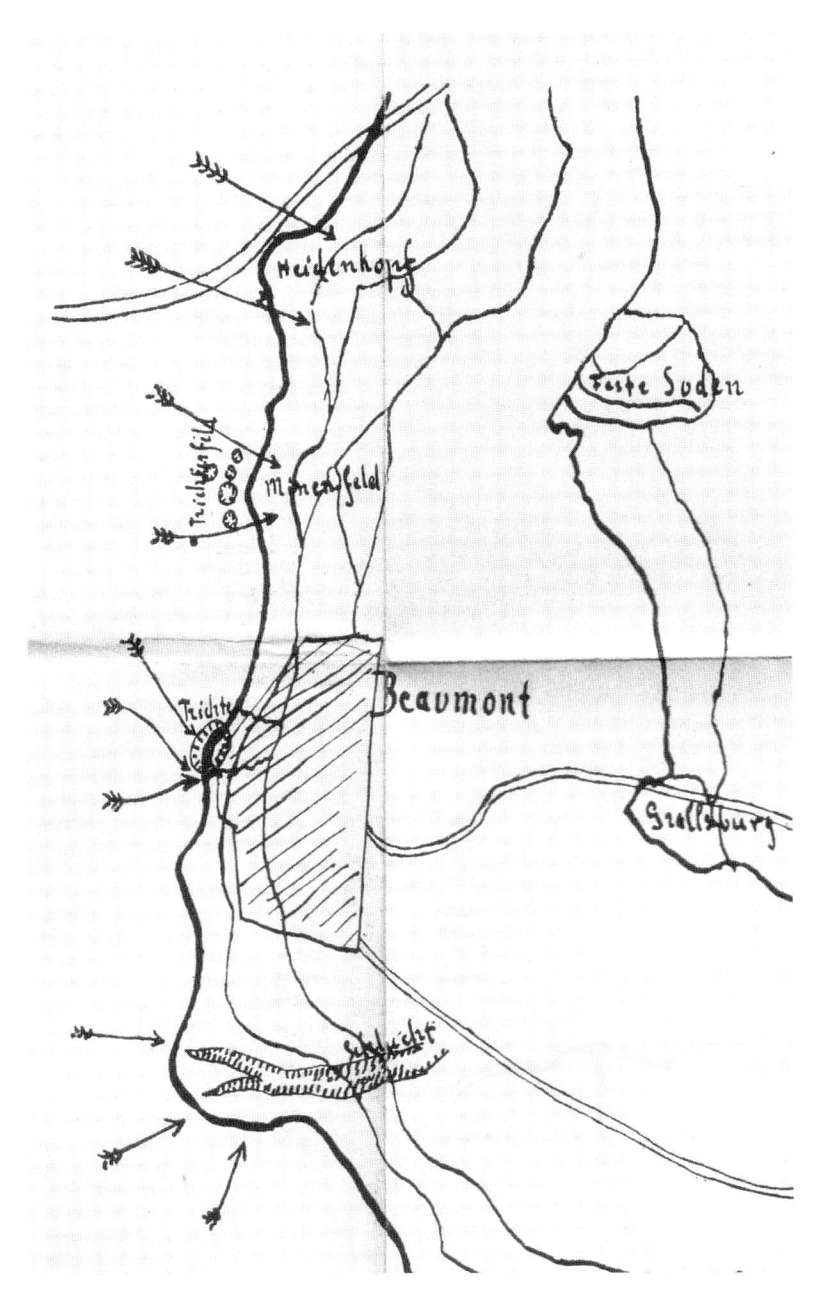

13. Sketch of the main British thrusts against 51 Reserve Brigade on 1 July 1916.

The wreckage of Beaumont Hamel after the seven-day bombardment.

terrible effect on the positions. The barbed wire obstacles, which had been laid with such effort in considerable depth in front of each of the trenches of the First Position, had largely been swept away by a combination of shrapnel fire and heavy trench mortars; the trenches were mere hollows in the ground, with craters overlapping craters; whilst the entrances to the dugouts were reduced to rough holes in the ground. Heavy shells had wrecked every single dugout on the 9th Company front. Beaumont Hamel itself was smashed beyond recognition. The cemetery, laid out in quieter times by the regiments which had occupied this sector, had disappeared off the face of the earth, as had the German memorial. The narrow gauge railway, which ran along the valley floor towards Beaucourt and up to the Leiling Stollen, was utterly wrecked and the valley itself was littered with dead horses, smashed wagons, broken branches, uprooted trees and all the debris of war.

Yet amidst all the chaos and confusion, courageous carrying parties still succeeded from time to time in getting through with water, rations and ammunition, despite the torrent of fire which caused them serious casualties. Furthermore, as the robust countering of the various raids had demonstrated clearly, the positions were still fully and effectively garrisoned by men who may have been suffering from thirst, hunger and lack of sleep, whose nerves may have been affected by the constant fear of being buried alive or meeting a violent end, but whose morale was essentially intact. There had been some casualties. Between 24 and 30 June, RIR 121 had lost twenty four killed, 122 wounded and one man missing; RIR 119 reported 20 dead and 83 wounded, but for the British this was a dismal return bearing in mind the many thousands of shells and tons of gas which had been directed at the defenders of this crucial area. 51 Reserve Brigade, its fighting capability virtually unimpaired, was fully ready for the life or death battle against the odds which was about to open. That this was the case was the clearest possible vindication of all the hard digging and other preparations that had been carried out during the past eighteen months. Now all the work, all the planning and all the training was to be put to the test.

Shelling continued throughout the night of 30 June – 1 July. Aware through prisoner interrogations, the statements of a deserter and intercepted telephone messages that the offensive was upon them, the defenders checked and rechecked their weapons and ammunition, maintained a careful watch to their front and waited for dawn. There was a slackening of artillery fire in the early hours; from the British trenches came all the sounds and bustle of final attack preparations but, as dawn broke on a beautiful summer's day, the bombardment increased to drum fire of unprecedented intensity from 6.30 am. Within minutes the entire forward positions were one seething mass of exploding shells, flying fragments, smoke and dust. Down in the dugouts, men fastened on their equipment, picked up their weapons and grenades and crouched on the stairs and in the entrances, ready to sprint into position the moment the barrage lifted to the rear.

Suddenly, at 8.20 am, (7.20 am British time; German time was one hour ahead) an enormous explosion occurred on Hawthorn Ridge as a massive twenty tonne mine, constructed in total secrecy by British engineers during the previous few months, blew up, taking over half of 1 Platoon, 9th Company RIR 119 with it. Adjacent dugouts were crushed or buried. Less than two sections of 9th Company were ready for immediate action. There was so much chalk strewn around that it seemed as though there had been a snow storm and, in the midst of it, was a gaping crater over fifty metres in diameter and twenty metres deep, steaming hot and giving off poisonous fumes. It should have been the start of an easy local victory for the British army, but was nothing of the kind. Simultaneously the VIII Corps artillery lifted onto depth targets. The start of the main attack was still several minutes away but, thoroughly alerted, the German defenders all along the 51 Reserve

Part of the wood in H6, west of Beaumont Hamel after the bombardment. Compare this with the photograph of the view from the sunken road under Walk 2, page 121.

Brigade front raced to occupy their defensive positions. Telephone messages were passed swiftly to the rear and red flares went up calling for artillery fire. Then suddenly whistles blew and, climbing out of their trenches, on came the British infantry: wave after wave, heading into a maelstrom of interlocking small arms fire. It is a myth that the heavily-laden men advanced all along the British front at a walk, carrying their rifles at the high port with bayonets fixed. Tactics varied according to local conditions. Nevertheless witnesses from RIR 119 stated later that the advance was in fact conducted slowly at points along their front.

In Beaumont South, which was the responsibility of 1st Battalion RIR 119, Sector B5, which was located opposite *Geologen-Graben* and just forward of the Circus, No Man's Land was very narrow and the wire obstacle had suffered badly during the bombardment. Here the British succeeded in entering the front line trench in a few scattered places. Well rehearsed battle drills were executed by the defenders. These isolated pockets of British attackers were assaulted frontally by the garrison of the second trench and rolled up from either side by the occupants of the first trench. Within minutes the attackers had been ejected and two Lewis guns had been captured. Down in the valley of the Ancre there were initially also minor incursions here and there. Decisive counter-action by specially trained hand grenade teams soon dealt with these, too. Thrown back, the attackers took cover in shell holes forward of the German lines, where they attempted to conduct a fire fight with defenders, but the odds were stacked against them. Not only was this part of No Man's Land covered by five artillery defensive fire zones and the fire of Albrecht mortars, it was also completely dominated by machine guns positioned on the slopes of the *Grallsburg* and *Feste Alt-Württemberg* to the north of Station Road. Total confusion reigned amongst the attackers, who were pinned down and unable to move. By mid-morning it was all over. Those British soldiers who could do so, had pulled back to their starting points. The remainder spent the day pinned down in their shell holes – the dead, the wounded and the merely trapped, unable to move until darkness fell many hours later.

A little further to the north in Sector B3, which is where *Leiling Schlucht* (Y Ravine) and the grounds of the Newfoundland Memorial are located, the slopes to the south of the ravine were simply one great killing field that morning. Even before the first attackers appeared, the trenches were fully manned; riflemen and machine gunners even having time to select optimum fire positions, to bring up extra ammunition and to be given last minute orders by their section and platoon commanders. A machine gun was located on a small knoll just to the north of the western tip of Y Ravine and within minutes of the attack beginning, machine guns were also being moved forward in Sector B4 to improve their fields of fire into B3. So much for the close defence of 2nd and 11th Companies, but the real damage was done by the dense network of machine guns located along Station Road, the *Steinbruch Stellung* (Quarry Position), the *Grallsburg*, *Geologen-Graben* (Geologist's Trench), *Hang Stellung* (Slope Position) and *Feste Alt-Württemberg* (Beaucourt Redoubt). On a clear day the slightest movement could be detected and fired upon from any of these locations and, to make matters worse, a pair of captured Belgian machine guns were also sited on a piece of high ground near St Pierre Divion where they could fire in enfilade along the frontage and entire depth of the German First Position from Sectors B3 to B7. The Battle Log of RIR 119 records that initially the defensive artillery fire was not terribly effective, but that it was not necessary to rely on that alone. For example, Sector B2 reported a battalion massing for an attack to its front at 8.40 am. The order when it came was short and very much to the point. 'Destroy them with machine gun fire!' it said.

Beaumont Hamel, photographed on 2 July 1916.

Destruction by machine gun fire sums up the day in this area. No matter what the tactics, no matter how heroic the attacking infantrymen were; whether they were members of the South Wales Borderers and the Border Regiment of the first wave, or the Essex Regiment and Newfoundland Regiment of the second, there was simply no way through these interlocking arcs of fire and all attempts to do so withered away very quickly. The proof of this is the modest amount of ammunition fired by individual guns that day. Up near Serre, from the Brewery Position at Thiepval and on Hill 110 near Fricourt, some guns are known to have fired 20,000 rounds or more on 1 July 1916. Of the weapons of the 2nd Machine Gun Company, RIR 119, responsible for short range defence from north of Beaumont Hamel to the Ancre, only one fired as many as 4,000 rounds and two others as few as 1,250 and 1,500 rounds respectively: within a comparatively short time there was simply nothing left to shoot at.

Following the explosion of the mine there was a scene of confused close-quarter fighting on Hawthorn Ridge. Not surprisingly, around the crater there was little initial resistance and some of the attackers managed to get right up to it. 3rd Platoon, 9th Company was occupying a large dugout nearby, whose entrances had all been blocked by the explosion, leaving just one small hole to daylight. A sentry at the head of the stairs laboured feverishly to enlarge the hole, but before he could do so one of the first of the attackers bayoneted him and he fell back dead at the feet of his platoon commander, Reserve Leutnant Breitmeier and his company commander Reserve Oberleutnant Anton Mühlbayer, who was killed later in the day as one of eight officers from RIR 119 who fell. (Mühlbayer is buried in Fricourt German Cemetery Block 3, Grave 306). Reacting instinctively, Vizefeldwebel Davidsohn shot his attacker in the face with a flare.

Grenade and smoke bombs were thrown down the stairs, accompanied by demands for the surrender of the occupants of the dugout. Confident that other defenders would come to their aid, the men of 3rd Platoon pulled further back into the dugout and waited in silence. The first group to intervene was the crew of Machine Gun No. 2 of 2nd Machine Gun Company, RIR 119 commanded by Unteroffizier Aicheler. The explosion of the mine had blown both gun and team sprawling into the bottom of their firing bay. By the time they resumed their fire position the nearest attackers had penetrated the German position and were only twenty metres away. The gun opened fire, but jammed after ten rounds. After this stoppage had been cleared only another ten rounds were fired before it jammed again. 'Back!' ordered Aicheler, grabbing the gun and rushing into the next traverse. Here the (unknown) stoppage was finally cleared and the gun began to fire at point blank range at the attackers, who fell dead and wounded into the trench. At that a second group of attackers closed in on the area of the crater, but it was brought under fire from both No. 2 gun and also No. 1 gun commanded by Unteroffizier Braungart, who had a perfect view down over the Beaumont Hamel-Auchonvillers road, the slopes below the crater and the open ground between the Sunken Road and the German front line.

The result was a slaughter. Before No. 1 gun had fired off its first 250 rounds, two officers with drawn swords and a complete wave of infantrymen had fallen. Observing that no German artillery fire was coming down in this area, No. 1 gun then engaged and destroyed all subsequent waves, including columns advancing in depth, at ranges of up to 950 metres. Meanwhile No. 2 gun, assisted by cross fire from RIR 121 from the *Bergwerk* (Mine) north of the road, concentrated on those attempting to close up to the crater itself. Their forward rush checked, the attackers attempted to take cover, but they were in full view and all were killed. About twenty dazed men from 9th Company gathered behind No. 2 gun, too stunned to do anything, but forceful leadership from a Vizefeldwebel (possibly Davidsohn), got them forward where they engaged the remaining attackers with hand grenades. Pressure built and some of the attackers attempted to pull back. This made them easy pickings for No. 2 gun, whose fire brought them all down. When the bodies were recovered later, six of them had been cut in two by the bursts of fire.

By this time, two platoons of 7th and 12th Companies RIR 119 [probably at least 120 men in all], accompanied by a pair of *Musketen* (Danish Madsen air-cooled, magazine-fed, light machine guns) had dashed forward from depth positions and occupied the near rim of the crater under the command of Mühlbayer and Breitmaier, who had emerged from their near-blocked dugout. No.2 gun joined them, engaging a Lewis gun in a position the far side of the crater and knocking it out after a further 500 rounds had been fired. A British aircraft joined in, dropping bombs on men of 12th Company RIR 119, but without causing any damage. Still the battle continued. Vizefeldwebel Eugen Mögle of 7th Company led an unsuccessful grenade assault against a group of British soldiers to the south of the crater. Another British Lewis gun firing at short range caused numerous casualties amongst the defenders, several of whom were shot through the head, before Unteroffiziers Hefl and Rapp of 12th Company silenced it with well-aimed rifle fire.

Off to a flank Landwehr Leutnant Blessing of 10th Company observed what was happening around the crater in B1. He swiftly assembled a hand grenade team, comprising Brause, Fauser, Hermann and Gottlieb Lutz and Kappelmann. Storming forward at their head, he launched himself at the intruders. Seeing this, Vizefeldwebel Mögle

Front line trench in B1 west of Beaumont Hamel after it had been repaired following the blowing of the mine on 1 July 1916.

relaunched his attack with a composite group from 7th and 12th Companies . (Having distinguished himself this day and in later fighting, Mögle was seriously wounded in the battle for Stuff Redoubt, near Grandcourt on 29 September. He died of his wounds the following day and is buried at Sapignies German Cemetery, Block 2, Grave 150).

A hand-to-hand battle developed, which ended with the destruction of the British force and the capture of a wounded lieutenant (He was not named, but was described by his captors as 'courageous'). With at least ten Maxims and Lewis guns operating within 100 metres of each other, the air was full of the crack of bullets. A Lewis gun team attempted to bring their gun into action only fifteen metres from the German lines. Seeing this, Schütze Hermann from Aichele's No. 2 gun rushed forward, killing the crew with his pistol, seizing the gun and returning with it to the trench. The situation was beginning to stabilise. Further buried dugouts were cleared, releasing more men from 9th Company , so gradually the defenders got the upper hand. There were several subsequent attempts by the British to storm forward towards Beaumont Hamel and Hawthorn Ridge, but they were all shot to pieces by the combined fire of 7th, 9th, 10th and 12th Companies, not to mention a machine gun allocated to 5th Company, RIR 121 which, firing from amongst the houses on the western edge of the village, totally dominated all movement in the valley leading out of Beaumont Hamel. By 11.30 am the entire battle had died away in this area.

The scene was almost beyond description. Lying in amongst the shredded wire obstacles, sprawled in the grass bleached by the chlorine of the numerous gas attacks during the bombardment, were hundreds of khaki-clad bodies, whilst around the crater which was encircled by the fallen of 7th, 9th and 12th Companies, the British dead were piled in heaps. Wreckage from destroyed dugouts was intermingled with the heaped up chalk and there was no sign of the commander of 1 Platoon, 3rd Battalion RIR 119, Leutnant Renz. Suddenly, between 1.00 pm and 2.00pm, a hole appeared in the ground next to the rim of the crater and Renz emerged with some of his men. His dugout had survived the explosion, but the entrances were deeply buried. Thanks to hours of ceaseless, frantic digging Renz lived to fight another day – just as his air was about to run out. He must have had one of the luckiest escapes of the day. Others were not so fortunate. RIR 119 had eight officers and ninety three men killed that day and also suffered 191 wounded.

As a postscript to the fighting around the crater, this was the location of one of the German humanitarian gestures during the afternoon. An English-speaking Landsturmmann named Schneider,

Hauptmann von Ziegesar, (2nd left) 4th Company, 1st Battalion RIR 121, killed in action in Nagelgraben during the bombardment. Standing to his front in this photograph, taken on 9 January 1916, are Gefreiters Sommer and Guberan, who have just received the Iron Cross First Class for gallantry on patrol. These were rare awards for junior ranks.

noticing that some of the 'dead' in front of the position were moving about, called to them in his perfect English to surrender and come in: they would be well treated. After some persuasion the offer was accepted, a group of soldiers carrying a seriously wounded lieutenant came over. Although the rescue operation itself was not fired on, this was never a truce in the full sense of the word. It was entirely local. A British battery kept a neighbouring company under fire throughout but, ignoring it, men of 9th Company RIR 119 went forward several times with unwounded British prisoners and succeeded in bringing in five officers and thirty one other ranks, all wounded, not to mention important documents which were found on the person of a captured adjutant.

There was nothing to compare with the Hawthorn Ridge mine on Redan Ridge, which was cloaked from end to end in dust and smoke, but many of the men of the forward companies of RIR 121, crouching in the entrances to their dugouts, felt and heard the explosion of the huge mine and also spotted the lift of the artillery fire to the rear. Immediately they raced out of their shelters and manned the parapet of their smashed trenches. The story of the day is quickly told. In the southern section of Redan Ridge nearest to Beaumont Hamel, the attackers from the British 4th Division were simply driven back without ever having set foot in the German positions. A little further north, there was a minor incursion near the junction between the 1st and 2nd Battalions RIR 121, but an immediate counter-attack by Hauptmann Consor and a small group of men swiftly ejected the attackers and the same was true elsewhere along the regimental frontage. With the exception of the *Heidenkopf*, the entire line had been restored within an hour of the offensive being launched.

As has been noted, the *Heidenkopf* was evacuated during the latter part of the bombardment. Its purpose was to dominate the dead ground just to the south of the Serre – Mailly road, but it was too difficult to defend to be viable in the event of determined attack. Instead mine galleries had been driven beneath it and a series of mines were charged; the idea being to blow up the attackers as they surged forward to occupy the minor salient. A few observers remained in position until the attack, but none lived to tell the tale; all were killed either in the final stages of the bombardment or during the initial assault. It is certain that the few observers were unable to pass any sort of warnings to those in rear because, contrary to German hopes, the British attack was launched left and right of the *Heidenkopf*, with the aim of capturing and controlling the high ground to the east of Serre. Under the cover of smoke, clouds of dust and the dead ground in the area, leading elements were able to close up to the German lines and in some cases enter them before the garrisons emerged from their dugouts. Vicious hand-to-hand fighting ensued, covered by machine gun and rifle fire from depth positions, which largely kept follow-up waves of attackers in check. Four mines were detonated beneath the *Heidenkopf* about fifteen minutes after the attack started, but although some casualties were caused to the British, the effect was nowhere near what had been expected. A subsequent engineer report concluded that the effort had largely been wasted; that the trap was too obvious.

There then began a desperate battle for control of Bayerngraben (Bavaria Trench) and its immediate surroundings. This lasted for some considerable time; grenade teams launching attacks from three sides, some of them over the top, until stocks of grenades began to run out. The stalemate was eventually broken about mid-morning, when reinforcements arrived from 3rd Battalion RIR 121 together with the platoon of Leutnant Hoppe from IR 169 to the north. With increased resources available to the defence and the move forward of British reinforcements and supplies across No Man's Land being prevented by constant artillery fire, it was possible to begin a sustained push aimed at restoring the entire front line, including the *Heidenkopf*. This was far from easy because the British defended obstinately, forming one block after another with their Lewis gun teams. Nevertheless progress was made gradually so that, as night fell, there was only one British pocket of resistance still holding out. This, too, was eventually eliminated and by 2 July RIR 121 was once more master of its original sector. Numbers of British soldiers managed to regain their own lines, but the remainder were captured, either on 1 July or the following day, when a detailed search of the *Heidenkopf* area and its numerous extensive dugouts yielded a total of 200 prisoners. Some members of RIR 121 had of course been captured and their losses had been fairly steep on 1 July. Altogether between 1 and 10 July 1916 the regiment lost 179 killed, 291 wounded and seventy missing, but most of these losses occurred on 1 July.

The *Heidenkopf* was a charnel house, a scene of utter devastation. Bodies, British and German, were strewn around everywhere, heaped up in places and intertwined. Abandoned and destroyed weapons and equipment lay all over the area. The regiment estimated that it had lost 150 men killed in the complex of trenches and that the British losses might have been as much as three times as great. Altogether the defenders counted 1,200 British dead in front of the 1st Battalion and

A quiet moment in the sunshine of August 1916 in Y Ravine. Notice that steel helmets have still not been issued at this point to men of RIR 119.

576 in front of the 2nd Battalion. They had also captured twenty eight machine guns, four mortars and an enormous quantity of ammunition and equipment ranging from digging tools to telephones.

Reserve Leutnant Beck of RIR 121 had a unique overview of the events during the bombardment and on 1 July in and around the *Heidenkopf*. He had been appointed battalion observer and was stationed in a one-man reinforced concrete cupola between the first and second trenches immediately in rear of the *Heidenkopf*. It is still possible to visit the remains of an observation post like this nearby. It is located just to the right of the track which leads from the Ulster Tower to St Pierre Divion at the 'Pope's Nose' in Sector C2.

> *Each morning at 5.00 am, I took up my position, he recalled vividly later, It was my duty to observe to my front, to locate the positions of machine gun posts, mortar pits and enemy battery positions. This information I passed on to the artillery forward observation officer, who spent some hours with me each morning. These locations were then engaged by the guns. It did not take the enemy long to spot my periscope and we were brought under especially heavy fire. The enemy trench system was located on the opposite slope, the far side of a slight dip. We noted an increasing number of trenches being dug left and right of the communications*

trenches. Their appearance left us in no doubt that the major offensive was about to be launched, because their only possible purpose was to house troops waiting to go into the attack.

The morning of 1 July arrived. Everything was enveloped in fumes and smoke. The drum fire, which had slackened to some extent, was mostly coming down on our batteries. As the visibility improved, I could see that the British trenches were overflowing with masses of troops. They stood there laughing and joking, some groups were having a quiet smoke, sitting on the parapet with all their equipment on. The enemy fire increased in intensity, reaching hurricane proportions towards 8.00 am. Suddenly it lifted onto our rear positions and we felt the earth shake violently – this was caused by a mine going off near Beaumont. In no time flat the slope opposite resembled an ant heap. Wave after wave of assaulting British troops hurled themselves forward through the dust and smoke towards our positions. I was just able to report the start of the attack to Battalion Headquarters then my rearward communications, my underground cable, was cut. Elements of the first British wave had worked their way forward very close to our positions under cover of the artillery fire and general obscuration. At once they overran the dugout on the left flank of 3rd Company, which was located immediately to the left of the evacuated Heidenkopf. Following up in strength, the enemy broke through and began to attack 3rd Company from the flank and rear. Courageously the company began at once to defend itself.

Desperately I fired off red flares calling for defensive fire which would interdict the further move forward of the masses of enemy. But only a few guns responded. Nevertheless, the advancing enemy was so thickly massed that every shell found its mark. Now I noticed the effect of some of the machine guns, which were cutting down the enemy in waves just like mowing machines. Their curtains of fire reached as far as Signy Farm, causing the British cavalry which was assembled there ready for the pursuit to turn away. Our somewhat primitive earth mortars also had an appalling effect, tearing great holes in the ranks of the British who were strolling happily forward. On one occasion I saw one of the barrel-like rounds curving up in a great arc to land next to a British section. The British stood stock still in surprise then one went over to see what it was and called the remainder to satisfy their curiosity. I could hardly have hatched a more diabolical plan if I had tried, because suddenly there was just a great black cloud there and *bodies were flying in all directions through the air. One of them, a tall Scot* [who must have been a member of 2nd Battalion Seaforth Highlanders] *came down on a steel post which had been part of our destroyed barbed wire obstacle and was spitted straight under his lower jaw. Thereafter I was faced with the gruesome sight of a death's head staring at me.*

In the meantime a patrol of British soldiers had made their way to my isolated cupola. The next few seconds would determine my fate. A strong group came to the entrance to my turret and bawled 'Germans?' No reply! Two hand grenades came flying in, but were trapped by the timber framework. They exploded wrecking the timber and doing my hearing no good. A second group was hard on their heels, but when they saw the damage to the dugout entrance paid it no more attention. To check on the situation I crawled out later and looked over the edge of a crater towards the rear. Not ten metres behind my cupola I saw a British outpost armed with a machine gun and radio equipment [sic. This seems to be a strange observation. A telephone would have been more likely, but Beck, admittedly writing some time after the event, specifically refers to a Funkapparat – radio equipment] *manning a sandbag wall. Instantly I disappeared once more and waited for darkness so I could break through to our lines under the cover of darkness.*

Just as it began to go dark there was a sharp exchange of artillery fire, which began to fall in my area. I made use of this to get past the British party. I crawled and slid across country towards the rear. Because I did not know how far the British had penetrated, I did not dare to speak or attempt to make contact with the occupants of a dug out until I reached Nagelgraben. Here I linked up with comrades from 12th Company and, when I discovered that the counter-attack was under way, I gathered a few comrades and headed off to deal with the block by my cupola. When we got to grenade-throwing range, we discovered that the job had already been done. The bodies of three dead British soldiers lay tangled up with the damaged machine gun and the radio equipment. I then raced forward to join my company in the front line trenches, which had been recaptured by 4th Company, supported by other companies of the regiment and a platoon of IR 169, our neighbouring regiment to the right.

Sitting amongst comrades from the other companies, tired out and emotionally drained, were the remnants of my 3rd Company – thirty men and five Unteroffiziers. They slumped there, dog tired and spent. It had all been too much! Oberleutnant Lutz, the company commander had been seriously wounded in the first moments of the attack... The three platoon commanders Reserve Leutnants Seidel, von Gaisberg and Bauer had all fallen, along with three quarters of the company during the counter-attack.

Despite being subjected to an unprecedented bombardment and determined attack, most of the frontage of 51 Reserve Brigade had not been penetrated at all and, where it had, every metre had been recaptured within a few hours. 1 July 1916 had been a long, dangerous and trying day for the brigade, but everywhere it had prevailed. It had been a triumph for the defence and a catastrophe for the attackers. For days the cries and groans of the wounded could be heard coming from No Man's Land, but despite all efforts very few could be found during the hours of darkness and recovered. Attempts were made from time to time by the British to arrange a truce, but the German defenders were concerned about the vulnerability of their positions in this area, were afraid of trickery and refused to negotiate when white handkerchiefs were waved. A heavy rainstorm four days later saw the emergence of the last of the British wounded who were able to crawl out of rain-filled shell holes forward of the *Heidenkopf.* As many of the remaining wounded men as possible were brought in, then at last; and far too late, a stillness descended on the front.

Chapter 6

THE FALL OF BEAUMONT HAMEL AND THE BATTLE FOR REDAN RIDGE NOVEMBER 1916

AFTER THE UNPRECEDENTED bloody reverse for the British army on 1 July, the Beaumont Hamel sector became a relatively quiet sector as the focus of the fighting switched: first to the area in the south of the Albert-Bapaume road then to the Ovillers Spur and Thiepval Ridge. It would be wrong, however, to assume that nothing happened between July and November 1916. There was constant artillery fire and patrol activity, which made the work of repair of the trenches difficult then, on 3 September 1916, an attack was launched between Beaumont Hamel and Thiepval as a diversion for the final assault on Guillemont. Once again obvious preparations meant that the attack was no surprise to 1st Battalion RIR 119, which was defending Sectors B4 to B7 down by the Ancre. After drum fire which began at 6.00 am, the attack by the British 39th Division ran straight into an almighty hail of artillery and small arms fire. Only in two places was any progress made. North of the river this was in Sectors B6 and B7, but counter-attacks pinched out the gains and by the evening of 3 September the entire line was once more secure. Casualties were inflicted on the attackers at a ratio of about 4:1, but the endless fighting and trickle of casualties had taken its toll. RIR 119 had been constantly in the front line without relief since May 1915, so two days later it was relieved by RIR 55. Gradually, with the arrival of IR 62 in late October, the defence which was to face the final test in the Beaumont Hamel area took shape.

Senior commanders had been aware for nearly a month that preparations were being made to renew the assault on the northern flank of the British sector of the Somme. Week by week the German army had observed the movement of reserves and increasing numbers of guns into the area and had even noted how in early November there was an artillery bombardment each morning around dawn. They identified it as an attempt to get the trench garrisons used to this pattern of activity, so that when one day it was followed by an actual infantry assault, surprise would be achieved. Given that that was the

British dead, killed during the diversionary attack on 3 September 1916.

case, it is reasonable to ask what counter-measures were taken to prepare for the forthcoming blow. The answer is quite simple: nothing at all was done to reinforce the area under threat and that simple fact underlines clearly the strain caused to the German army during the recent months of fighting. The continuous losses were beginning to have an effect on their ability to put up an effective defence.

At the end of October, 12th Infantry Division had been deployed to the Beaumont Hamel area. It was a shadow of the formation which had fought so hard and taken such punishment at the beginning of the battle, a fact which goes a long way to explain why, when the attacks were launched, the defence was far less effective than it had been on 1 July. RIR 55 had been defending Beaumont South from Sector B4 south to the Ancre since early September. IR 62 was now inserted into Sectors H5 and H6 (due west of Beaumont Hamel village) and B1 – B3, which stretched down south roughly as far as the eastern tip of *Leiling Schlucht* (Y Ravine). Redan Ridge was the responsibility of IR 23, which had relieved RIR 121 on 7 November. All the companies were very under strength and worn down by the bad weather. Coughs and colds were universal. IR 62 was deployed as follows: H5, H4, B1, B2 and B3 were held by 1st, 3rd, 11th, 10th and 9th Companies respectively. 4th and 12th Companies were in the second line of trenches, 2nd and 5th Companies in the third, with 6th, 7th and 8th back in the *Artillerie Mulde* (Artillery Hollow) north of Beaucourt, ready to move forward as required. There had been little action in this sector during the previous weeks, so the companies took over obstacles and positions which were in fairly good condition. There were still plenty of good deep and dry dugouts, for example. This was just as well because there was a great deal of artillery fire at night, reaching right back to the east of Beaucourt, as the Allies sought to make life as difficult as possible for the defence as the day of the attack drew closer.

By now the battlefield presented an appalling sight. Nothing green was to be seen. Craters overlapped craters from horizon to horizon. The dull brown of the mud was made greyer by the leaden skies of November. A more dismal landscape can barely be imagined. The roads, tracks and pathways were ploughed up or had disappeared. In consequence the task of the carrying parties was almost impossible and provision of water, rations and ammunition became extremely erratic. It was still possible to get motor transport forward as far as Puisieux. Thereafter, with the help of a light tramway, onward movement was possible as far at the *Artillerie Mulde*. After that it was a matter of carrying everything forward via the *Kriegsminister-Graben* (Minister of War Trench) and *Ziegesar-Graben* (named after Hauptmann Freiherr von Ziegesar, commanding officer 1st Battalion RIR 121 until his death in late June 1916). From the eastern edge of Beaumont Hamel, there were no really clearly defined trenches any more and carriers had to struggle forward in mud knee deep from crater to crater; an utterly exhausting procedure. Small wonder that the two forward battalions reported constantly that they were short of rations, ammunition and flares. To cap it all, heavy rain set in, rendering several areas totally impassable and the forward troops had to labour constantly to stop mud flowing down into the dugouts.

So the days wore on. The artillery fire increased in intensity, directed by observers in low-flying aircraft, which also attacked and machine gunned any of the defenders who showed themselves above ground by day. By 7 November the positions, the trenches and the wire obstacles were largely destroyed or swept away. Casualties mounted, signallers laboured incessantly to try to maintain telephone lines and exhausted runners attempted to keep information flowing backwards

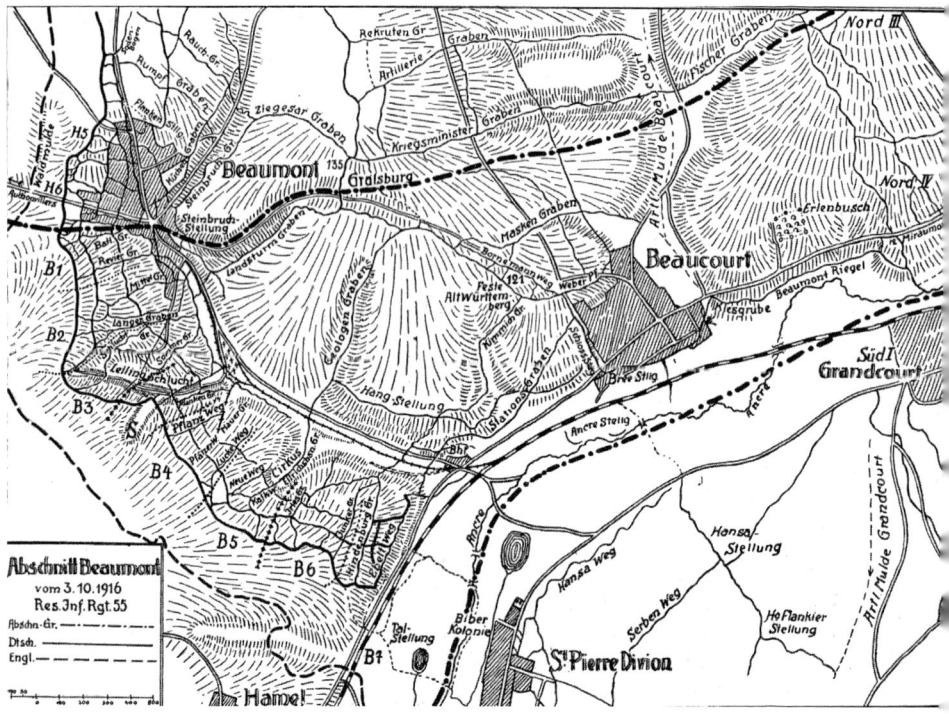

14. Map of Beaumont South October 1916 after RIR 55 had relieved RIR 119.

and forwards, despite the wrecked trenches and deep mud. Attempts were made with some success to suppress British machine guns and mortars, but there was insufficient artillery available to gain dominance and the defenders had to sit it out in their dugouts, ready to react in the event of an attack. During the nights, Allied patrols probed forward or attempted to raid the forward trenches, but these minor offensive operations were generally driven off without difficulty and were countered by such means as the raid launched by 1st Battalion IR 62 during the night 9/10 November, when a double sentry position was wiped out, British trenches were entered and grenades were thrown into numerous dugouts. The British trenches contained a large number of casualties, dead and alive, but difficult ground conditions meant that none could be recovered and the raid withdrew having lost three men.

Earlier British advances along the Thiepval ridge meant that long stretches of the German first position between Y Ravine and the Ancre could be engaged in enfilade by the guns. By 10 November, IR 62 had lost 38 men killed and 134 wounded. These losses were significant, bearing in mind that the regiment went into the line with company strengths of only eighty to ninety all ranks. 9th Company, located in the south next to RIR 55, had suffered particularly heavily, especially during the afternoon of 12 November, when an entire platoon was overcome by the effects of a particularly heavy bombardment with gas shells, but there was no means of relieving it. 2nd Battalion IR 62 had to be kept in reserve and used to find carrying parties. Those holding the front line just had to stick it out. Almost all of them were ill with colds, laryngitis and stomach complaints, made worse by the erratic arrival of poor quality rations and the fact that their clothing and boots were constantly soaked through. The whole regiment ought to have been relieved without further delay, but there were no reinforcements to be had. Warnings of an imminent attack kept arriving throughout 11 and 12 November and the garrison hung on grimly, heartened somewhat by the fact that a relative lull in the artillery fire permitted the move forward of a large amount of rations and ammunition.

Finally, on 13 November, the period of high alert came to an end. The previous night had been unusually quiet. The rain had cleared and an almost full moon shone down on the battlefield. It was possible to observe a long distance, but although things appeared to be quiet, the defenders were suspicious that something might be about to happen. Unluckily for them, just before dawn, thick fog, which had been a feature of the past few mornings, descended once more, reducing visibility drastically. The number of sentry positions and flare relay points was increased. At 6.00 am all was still, but at 6.45 am drum fire was opened all along the German front line. Almost simultaneously there was a massive explosion as a mine exploded once more under Hawthorn Ridge, taking many men from 11th Company IR 62 with it and wrecking a large section of the front line. At that the British charged forward and the outcome was in sharp contrast to the fiasco of 1 July.

Fähnrich Pukall of 3rd Company was manning the front line trench with his men, during the moments leading up to the assault. He had a grandstand view of the mine as it exploded.

'The mist was very thick and all was noticeably quiet. I went towards the hollow, where the double sentry post reported, 'Terrible fog, but all's quiet!' I then went back to the left flank, where Geisemeyer, who always was a very acute observer, called me over and urged me to listen, because something was happening out there today. I listened intently and could hear repeated muffled sounds. It

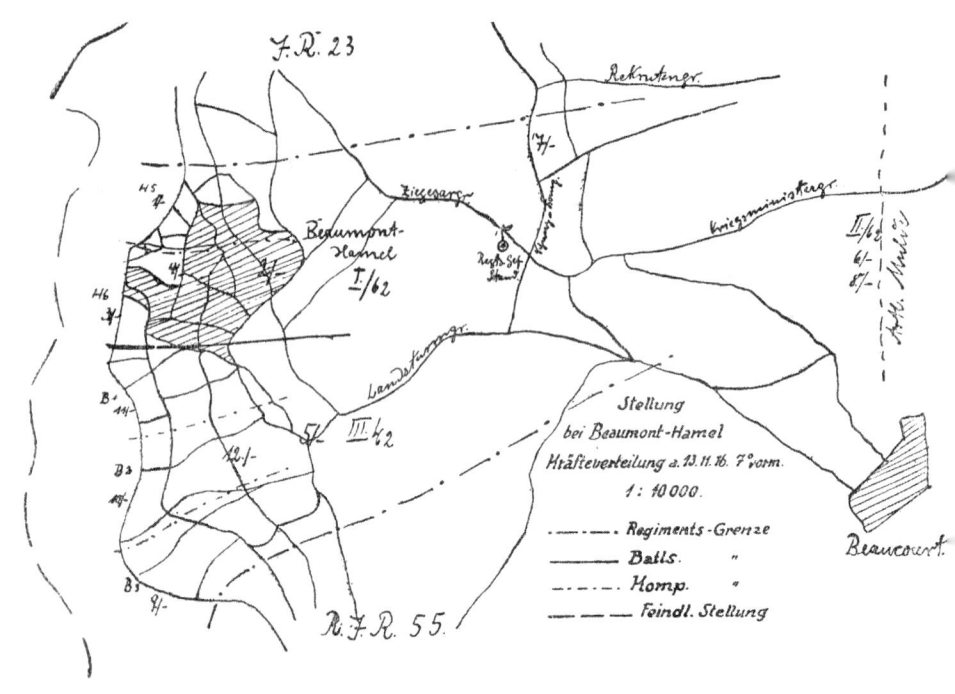

15. Sketch of the defensive areas of responsibility around Beaumont Hamel on 13 November 1916.

could not be digging or wire cutters; the British must be moving forward! I stood my platoon to and dashed over to the right flank, where the same sounds could be heard. 'Stand to!' I ordered. 'Maintain high alert!'...It was essential to act before the Tommies did. I had to blow the mine and get the machine gun bringing fire down to the front. Why was the machine gun in the hollow not firing? I ran towards the hollow then, horrified, I staggered back a few paces. What was that? A huge pillar of flame and smoke was ascending skywards. The mist distorted and magnified its extent, making its exact location and size impossible to judge. Simultaneously a hail of machine gun fire was opened along the front, and mortar bombs rained down amongst clouds of shrapnel. I raced back to my platoon. The sentries dived for cover – Attack!'

As the echoes of the mine blast died away, the defence reacted as best it could in the generally unfavourable circumstances. As the fire lifted the defenders raced to man their parapets, greeting the advancing troops with a hail of rifle and machine gun fire and showers of grenades. The critical difference, apart from the physical size of the garrison, was the lack of visibility due to the fog. The really serious damage in and around Beaumont Hamel in July was caused by long range machine gun fire and later accurate artillery defensive fire. On this murky morning, with visibility measured in a few metres, the fighting was all at short range. As a result, the front line trenches were penetrated in several places. However the defence had been arranged in depth as far as possible, so in addition to those places where the initial attacks had been halted and checked with heavy losses, for a while the defenders held their own – even taking some British soldiers prisoner. For a short while there was no sign of reinforcement for the attackers and the men of IR 62 felt that, all things considered, they had acquitted themselves well. Suddenly the sound of battle was heard from the rear. As the fog began to lift the cause became clear. There had been a breakthrough to the south in the RIR 55 area and another penetration in and around the eastern tip of *Leiling Schlucht* (Y Ravine), held by the weak 9th Coy IR 62. Loud shouts and battlecries in English could be heard as the attackers, swinging round to the north closed up on the village.

The main force of this attack had come in against B5 and B4. A further contingent of the 63rd (Royal Naval) Division skirted the flooded area along the Ancre, where all contact with RIR 95 had been lost days earlier, then swung north. Within a very short time, B6 was outflanked, all telephone links to the rear were severed, the *Kolonie* (Colony) had fallen and with it the command structures of 1st and 3rd Battalions RIR 55. The commanding officers Hauptmann von Obernitz (1st Battalion) and Major Tauscher (3rd Battalion) went straight into captivity, together with several other officers holding key appointments. Flares sent despairingly upward calling desperately for artillery support went largely unseen and unanswered. At platoon and company level the front line troops did what they could, held out as long as possible, but they were simply overwhelmed. The visibility was hopeless, the command structure had fallen apart and, with no communication, no support or reinforcements could be deployed in a coordinated manner. The inevitable consequence was a crumbling of the hitherto solid defences of the area.

Lest the German defenders appear to have given up too readily, it must be remembered that RIR 55 had been in the line for no less than ten weeks without a break at this point. They had endured all that bad weather and constant bombardment could throw at them, but to hold a major attack was probably asking too much of them. Blame, if it can be legitimately apportioned, probably should be laid at the door of the

High Command. It was well known that the obstacle belt had been largely swept away and had only been partially replaced in some places by knife rests and other temporary structures. The troops were exhausted, worn down by the privations they had suffered over so many weeks, yet nothing was done about it. Nevertheless, as Allied accounts of the battle relate, the defenders fought as hard as they could and as long as they could; the extremely high casualties bear witness to this fact.

Soon, however, there began a chaotic hand-to-hand struggle in and around the eastern edge of Beaumont Hamel, where the 3rd Company and staff of 1st Battalion IR 62 found themselves engaged by a strong force of British soldiers. Men from both sides were captured briefly then released as reinforcements arrived. Some also managed to escape. One such was Reserve Leutnant Hofmann, adjutant 1st Battalion IR 62. Whilst being led away as a prisoner, he attacked his escort, overcoming him and tearing his rifle out of his hands. Bleeding profusely from a chest wound, he fought his way back to regimental headquarters, only to die later of his wounds. Reserve Leutnant Römer and six men managed a similar feat, but these were exceptions to the rule during that confused day of fighting. Telephone communications were cut immediately the drum fire came down and that fact, coupled with the fog, made command and control exceedingly difficult for the regimental commander, Oberstleutnant von Poser, who, his own headquarters directly threatened with being overrun, rushed forward with a small group to the Intermediate Position at 7.15 am in order to try to restore order from chaos.

An early attempt to go to the aid of the two forward battalions with elements of the 2nd Battalion IR 62, which had been called forward from the *Artillerie Mulde* (Artillery Hollow), Beaucourt had to be abandoned; there were simply too many British soldiers already established in the intervening area. Instead the men were used to prevent the attack from being pressed to the north via the *Grallsburg* towards *Feste Soden* (Soden Redoubt). Further attempts to make contact forward with troops fighting in and around the village failed for lack of numbers. Contact was made to the north with elements of IR 23, but all links to RIR 55 were lost. Patrols were despatched to try to rectify this, initially without success, because *Feste Alt-Wüttemberg* (Beaucourt Redoubt), where its headquarters had been located, had already been lost. Eventually, late in the afternoon, contact was made. Meanwhile fighting went on forward in and around Beaumont Hamel throughout the morning and some particularly courageous groups barricaded themselves into small nests of resistance and held out until at least 4.00 pm, surrendering only when they had run out of ammunition and all chance of a relieving counter-attack had disappeared.

Writing from captivity, Rittmeister von Dresky, 3rd Battalion IR 62, sent his regimental commander a vivid description of the fighting for Beaumont Hamel that day.

At 6.45 am there was a powerful enemy explosion in Sector B1, which blew up or buried a platoon of 11th Company IR 62. At the same moment, extraordinarily heavy drum fire came down on Beaumont Hamel. A few moments later the entire battalion frontage was under attack, but everywhere our rifle and machine gun fire caused heavy casualties. Where the mine had gone off the enemy was able to break in to our front line. Whilst the companies were engaged in holding off the frontal attacks of the enemy, large detachments of enemy soldiers, coming from the direction of Beaucourt, advanced along Mittleren-, Revier-, Grenz- and Karren-Graben (Centre, Aid Post, Border and Wheelbarrow Trenches), towards our position and attacked the companies from the rear. Having suffered heavy losses, by 9.30 am the companies had to surrender Sectors B1 and B2. In Sector B3, having defeated the first enemy attack, 12th Company IR 62 launched a counter-attack under Reserve Oberleutnant Holle. Thirty six prisoners were captured along with a machine gun and a mortar, but Oberleutnant Holle was killed. With his passing, the battalion lost an outstandingly courageous and energetic officer

When 12th Company was attacked from the rear, it went into all-round defence and fought on until 4.00pm. By then, reduced to a strength of about three sections (less than thirty men), the remnants had to surrender. In the third line trench, 5th Company IR 62 fought bravely under Leutnant Hopf until 2.00 pm. The battalion staff alerted all the remaining reserves as soon as the attack began. By 7.00 am the first of the British soldiers appeared near the battalion command post, but they were driven off with small arms fire, taking cover in a dugout which housed the battalion medical officer, Doctor Schuhmacher and twenty wounded men. Vizefeldwebel Christoph and Fähnrich Dinter launched a grenade attack against these attackers, prevented them from advancing further for the time being, but were themselves wounded during the course of the fighting. Attempts to contact the forward companies by runners all failed; none of the runners despatched ever made it back to the battalion command post. However Unteroffizier Drzenga and two men of 11th Company IR 62 did succeed in fighting their way through to the battalion command post with a report. At about 9.30 am enemy detachments were seen advancing from the direction of Beaucourt. A machine gun manned by Unteroffizier Nietsch was brought into action and fired at these enemy soldiers with good success until around 11.45 am. By then the enemy had brought up fresh troops, who dug in hastily to the east of Beaumont Hamel and brought machine guns into action. The command post also came under fire from the north about this time. Completely surrounded, the command post had to be surrendered at about 12.45 pm, when an attack by about 200 British soldiers led by an Irish captain launched a final attack at it.

Meanwhile the situation was far from rosy in the Intermediate Position. Its forward battalions were smashed and out of the fight, so IR 62 was reduced to the remnants of three companies and a digging company (probably no more than 300 riflemen) and there were no reserves immediately to hand. Throughout the night the Intermediate Position was probed by strong British patrols, but without success. As dawn broke on 14 November, the approach of masses of British reserves could be seen as they advanced between Auchonvillers and Beaumont Hamel. Towards midday a further attack was launched, but was beaten off by small arms fire and during the afternoon the first of the reserves began to arrive from the recently relieved 26th Reserve Division – one company of RIR 99, which was immediately deployed in support of RIR 55, because there was a great threat of a breakthrough near to Beaucourt, when the *Schloss Stellung* (Chateau Position) had had to be abandoned the previous day.

IR 23 had spent a difficult few days on Redan Ridge since assuming responsibility for the sector from RIR 121. The filthy weather and heavy bombardment had wrecked the position from end to end. The dugouts in this area were never as effective as the deeply mined ones south of Beaumont Hamel and the regiment began taking casualties as soon as it took over the cratered positions. Aided by a scattering of *Musketen* and with enormous difficulty, it organised itself for defence during the night 11/12 November as follows: H1 – two platoons 9th Company; H2 – two platoons 12th Company; H3 – 4th Company; H4 – 2nd Company; second trench in sectors H1-H4 – one platoon each from 9th and 12th Companies; *Röhlergraben* – 4th Company; *Brettauerweg* – one platoon 12th Company; *Nagelgraben* – 1st Company; *Sodenbogen* and *Geschwindgraben* – 3rd Company;

Intermediate Position behind H3 and H4 – 5th Company; *Feste Soden* – 7th Company; Nord I (depth positions) – 6th and 8th Companies. To say that the troops were thinly spread is barely to do justice to how scattered and lacking in mutual support they were. Nevertheless it was really the only feasible plan that the commander could devise and the companies settled down to make the best of it. There were not too many casualties from artillery fire that night despite all the re-deployments, but the following day the fire became so intense that no food could be delivered forward. In pouring rain the troops stayed on the alert, looking grimly at where their wire should have been. It had completely disappeared from the forward positions and nearly so from the Intermediate Position.

Apart from heavy artillery fire in the early morning of 13 November, the forward companies were reporting nothing out of the ordinary, until the 3rd Battalion heard the sound of the mine going off on Hawthorn Ridge, accompanied by the noise of small arms fire. At that moment its sector was hit by salvoes of gas shells, followed up by an assault, during which the 3rd Battalion positions in H1 and H2 were penetrated. A swiftly-organised counter-attack by 10th and 11th Companies restored the position by midday. 300 prisoners were taken and one machine gun was captured. Both 9th and 12th Companies had suffered heavily, so 10th and 11th Companies remained forward to reinforce the threatened area. There had also been problems further north. Shortly after 7.00 am, H3 reported, 'Enemy infantry attack on H3. Leutnant May has been severely wounded and carried down into a dugout'. This was followed up a few moments later by, 'The British have broken through on the right flank of H3. They are already in the second trench'.

The situation was thoroughly confused. The 1st Battalion staff burned important documents, dismantled telephone links and prepared to fight for their position. To their front the sound of small arms fire could be heard clearly. Flares were going up along the front of H3 and H4 calling for artillery fire, but the situation was thoroughly confused in the fog. Going forward, Hauptmann Eichholtz, the battalion commander, discovered that there were narrow penetrations at various points along the front. He decided, therefore, to order the remaining defenders to ignore the British barrage which was falling between the First and Intermediate Positions and to pull back to the latter, where it would be easier to make a decisive stand. By 9.00 am, Hauptmann Eichholtz was back in the Intermediate Position and taking a firm grip of the defence which was being conducted primarily

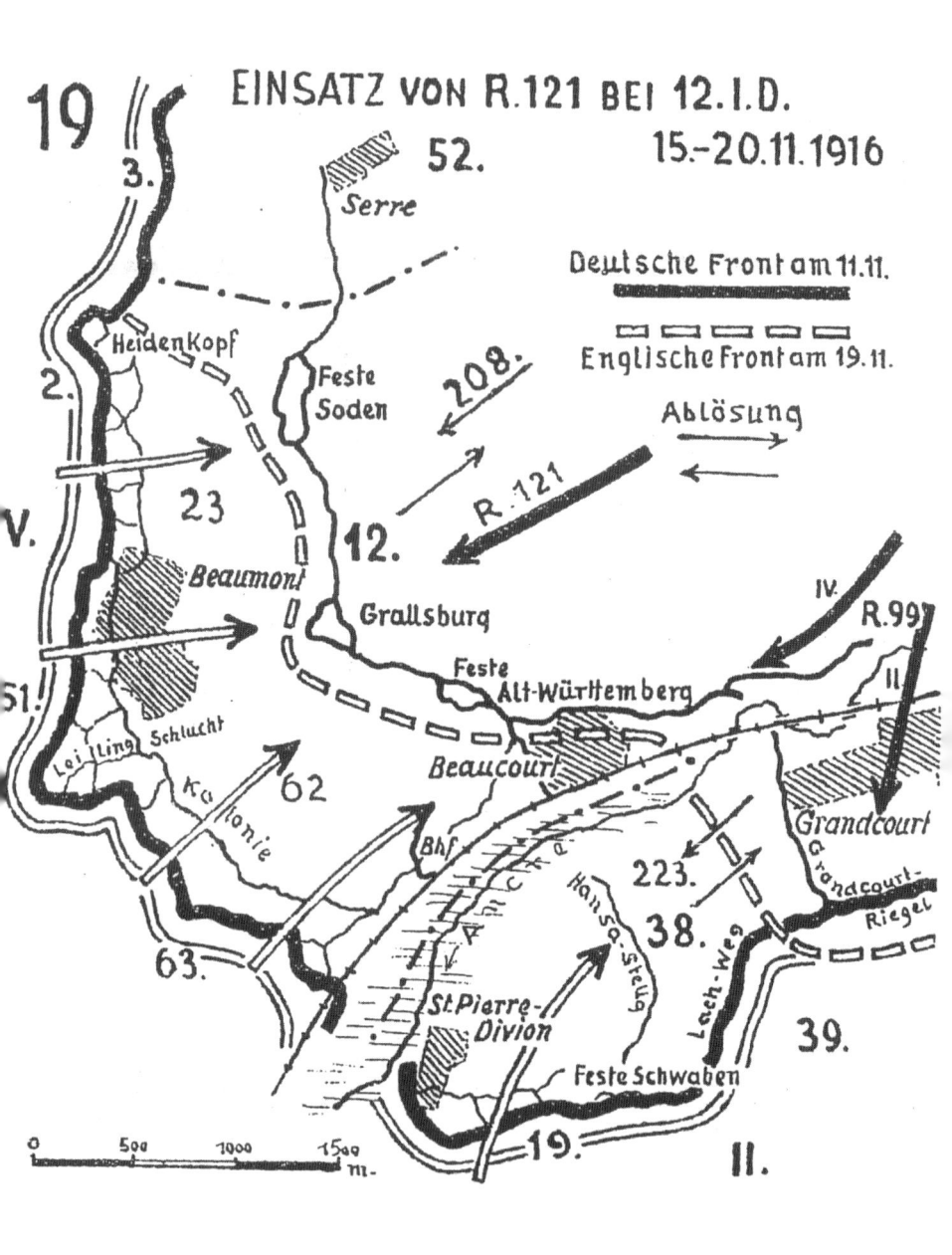

16. Ground gained and lost during the Battle of the Ancre November 1916.

by 7th Company and a digging company from a recruit depot. A threat had developed to *Feste Soden* in the fog, but prompt work by grenade teams from 5th and 7th Companies soon cleared the attackers away from this vital point.

As the day wore on there were repeated attempts by the British to gain ground the length of Redan Ridge. Some defenders from 3rd Battalion IR 23 were still holding out forward in H1 and H2 and were in contact with IR 169 on their right, but further south the *Heidenkopf* had fallen and British units were swarming all over the area between there and *Feste Soden*. There was a further attempt to attack the latter at around 4.00 pm, but it was stopped and small groups driven back from the web of trenches to its west. Further operations disputing possession of this ground was a recurrent feature of the battle during the next few days. Resupply was extremely problematic at this time; there was little ammunition and a great shortage of grenades, then the supply of clean water failed completely from 14 November, condemning the defenders to drink filthy, polluted water from the shell holes and leading, unsurprisingly, to an immediate increase in cases of illness. Despite the constant pressure on the Intermediate Position in general and *Feste Soden* in particular, the defence generally held firm. There were exceptions. The use of tanks against H1 and H2 on 15 November threatened to cut off the survivors of 3rd Battalion, who pulled back into the IR 169 area near Serre and consolidated there once more in a blocking position forward, to protect that regiment's left flank from being rolled up. Nevertheless, despite heavy casualties on both sides, the fighting or, rather floundering in the mud, that day was largely indecisive.

Amidst all the fighting *Feste Soden* held out as a cornerstone of the defence. Frequently threatened, bombarded, attacked and partially outflanked, thanks to its natural strength and the fact that it occupied a reverse slope position to attacks from the west meant that it was never taken and was only given up during the general withdrawal to the Hindenburg Line the following year. Much of the credit for this stubborn defence during these early days was given to Hauptmann Illgner, commanding officer of 2nd Battalion IR 23, who provided decisive leadership and, with indefatigable energy, was constantly at the point of danger, providing an inspiring and self-sacrificial example to all. Gradually over a period of days and, typically for the Battle of the Somme, reinforcements from RIR15, RIR 121, IR 63 and IR 173 were found, arrived in dribs and drabs and were fed into the battle, providing much-needed relief for the IR 23 companies, which had been bearing the brunt of the pressure throughout the battle. In fact, during the night 15/16 November 12th Infantry Division had been relieved by 208th Infantry Division (IR 25, RIR 65 and IR 185), but the situation on the ground was very much more complicated, with reliefs still incomplete forty eight hours later in some cases. By 17 November, for example, 8th Company IR 23 was down to three Unteroffiziers and eight men still able to fight and other sub units were not in much better condition, but some were still deployed. The remnants of IR 62 were not finally relieved by 1st and 2nd Battalions IR 25 until 20 November.

This confusion of formations, units and sub-units and intense command and control difficulties on Redan Ridge probably explains one of the strangest incidents of the entire battle, which was played out in a sea of muddy desolation from 18 to 25 November, when a party of around 120 men from 16th Battalion Highland Light Infantry and 11th Battalion Border Regiment, together with a few men from 2nd Bn King's Own Yorkshire Light Infantry, broke through the German front line in some strength, then held out in a stretch of what the British referred to as Frankfurt Trench. This actual location appears to have been part of the depth of the Intermediate Position on the northern section of the *Grallsburg*, somewhere between *Kriegsministergraben* (Minister of War Trench) and *Artilleriegraben* (Artillery Trench). The British perspective on this incident, which is comprehensively described by Michael Renshaw in the **Battleground Europe** guide *Redan Ridge*, has passed into history as an heroic tale of endurance (which it certainly was) and a week-long battle against the odds. The German accounts of the incident, of which there are at least two in the regimental histories and another derived from them, suggest strongly that the cock up theory of history was hard at work on the heights above Beaumont Hamel that week.

The first description is taken from the history of Infantry Regiment 185 from Baden. Its history is laid out in diary form. This passage is taken from the entries for 24 and 25 November 1916:

The British Nest Episode

This episode shows how difficult it was to fight in a monotonous cratered landscape whose shape changed hourly. Trench lines could no longer be made out, dugouts were hard to spot and orientation was extraordinarily difficult. On 18 November British troops, who had broken through in a strength of approximately two companies, had occupied dugouts whose existence was not known to the regiment, about 300 metres behind the German front line. Initially they remained hidden by day and took passing individuals prisoner. Then, on the 23rd, they were discovered by a patrol from 12th Company, which was searching the area for British stragglers. They had even succeeded in making contact with their own troops by means of a gap in the German front line which had been kept open by British aircraft. As a result a failed attempt was made on the 23rd to rescue them.

Once the 'Nest' was discovered, 3rd Battalion IR 185 took immediate steps to deal with them, without knowledge of their strength, however. As a result, on the 24th a thirteen man patrol under Leutnant Geppert from 12th Company IR 185, worked its way forward to a dugout, capturing a machine gun, but being forced to pull back in the face of these strong enemy forces, having taken casualties. An attack during the afternoon failed, because the 10th Company which was cooperating missed the objective. The 5th Company IR 185 also failed on the morning of 25 November. In the meantime the British had become worn down and offered no resistance during the afternoon when an energetic attack was launched by 7th, 9th, 11th and 12th Companies IR 185. Four officers and about 160 [sic] men were taken prisoner, along with a machine gun, which could have cause enormous damage if initiative had been shown, for example, during the attack on the 23rd November. Ten German prisoners were freed. The Army High Command honoured the regiment on 26 November by mentioning its deeds in its report for that day.'

The second version of events is taken from the history of RIR 15:

There remains one remarkable incident; one which really typified the end of this long battle. During these days a noticeably large number of men carrying rations disappeared, so the men up front, who were suffering badly from the wet conditions, had to go without food. The whereabouts of these people was a mystery. Then a rumour started up that they had been grabbed by the Tommies during the pitch black night as they made their way forward. It was said that 1,000 Tommies had broken through and that they were occupying a section of trench. Reconnaissance then showed that there was a nest of Tommies between the First and Second Positions – which also explained the endlessly circling British aircraft over one section of trench. The Tommies had to be ejected immediately by means of a night operation but, under the direction of a guide who apparently knew the area, they stumbled around for eight hours during a rainy night, until eventually the unlucky Gefreiter broke down in tears, declaring that he had no idea where he was. As dawn broke it became clear that the whole group had gone round in circles and had arrived back at their starting point. Now the capture of the Tommies was carefully planned and prepared for the next night but one, when two complete battalions would be used. Completely surrounded the enemy surrendered before even a hand grenade battle was necessary. There was a captain, three other officers and 110 other ranks. They had hung on for eight long days, eating only food they had taken from our ration carriers. At the end of their strength, they wearily dragged themselves past us and into captivity. We watched them, not without high regard. Towards the end the iron-willed captain [presumably Captain Welsh, 11th Battalion Border Regiment] had apparently only prevented them from deserting by threatening them with his revolver. The entire affair was marked by confusion on both sides. One prisoner stated that his colonel had said before the attack, 'This is the final effort! Make sure that you capture some ground and that's it for this year!' In fact the battle was extinguished like a burnt out volcano which had spewed out the last of its lava. The expenditure of strength in the mud and cold was too great. Sickness reached significant proportions and the troops lost their drive.

The final sentences of the RIR 15 report have the ring of truth about them. The Battle of the Somme did not so much end as fizzle out, drowned and choked by the ubiquitous clinging mud and the foul weather. Perhaps it was appropriate that Beaumont Hamel, which was the high water mark of the 1914 advance, should also be the place where the Allies' endeavours reached their culminating point in the autumn of 1916, but to this day it remains desperately sad that such large numbers of brave men from both sides had to die for possession of an obscure little village of no strategic significance whatsoever.

Chapter 7

WALKS AND CAR TOUR

Whenever you park your car and leave it you are providing an opportunity for thieves. It is a sad fact that throughout Europe there are ne'er-do-wells who prey on tourists and visitors and the Somme is no exception. Petty thieves are well aware that those coming from abroad are likely to be carrying valuable items in their vehicles and it only takes a few moments for them to strike. Often it is not so much the intrinsic value of the items that is so annoying; rather it is the sheer aggravation of having to waste part of your valuable visit reporting losses to the police, credit card companies etc. If you are staying locally, secure your valuables in your accommodation and on no account leave passports or other documents, handbags or wallets in your vehicle, even if you are getting out for only a few minutes. Personally I park my car in Beaumont Hamel village near the church when I am visiting this area and I have never had any problems. I suggest that you do the same, but of course it is a matter of personal judgement.

If your mobility is restricted, it is possible with care to visit most of the places of significance by vehicle, but be careful. The mud of the Somme has not become less slippery over the years. It is very easy, even in a 4x4, to misjudge it. If your tarmac surface comes to an end and the weather is anything but bone dry, think very carefully before you drop your wheels onto a field. It is often better to reverse for hundreds of metres than to risk it, unless you want to get very muddy or spend a lot of time trying to persuade a farmer to pull you out.

View from German First Position, back towards Geologengraben and the Grallsburg where many depth machine guns were sited.

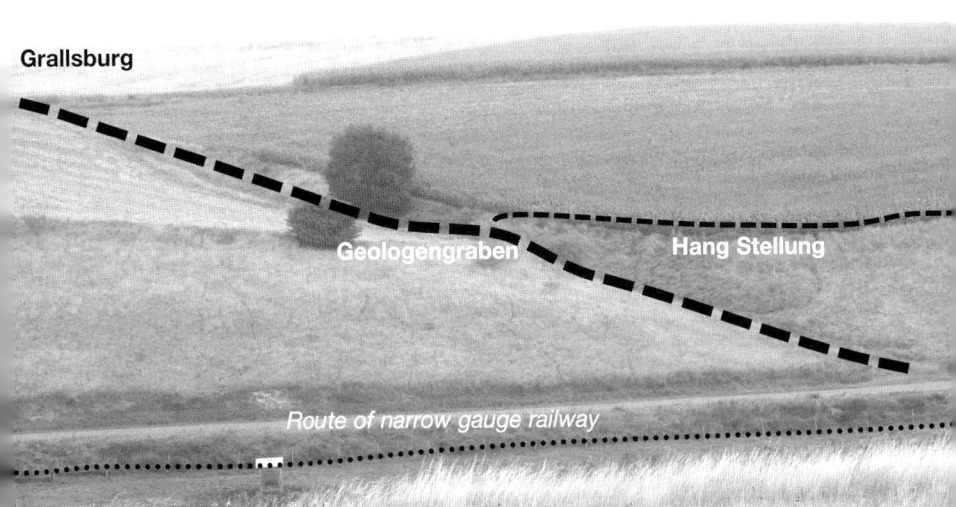

Walk 1:
Circus, Y Ravine, Newfoundland Memorial and Hawthorn Ridge
This walk takes approximately two hours; three if a visit to the Newfoundland Memorial is included.

Park your car near the church in Beaumont Hamel and head southeast down Station Road in the direction of Beaucourt, walking straight past the CWGC sign to the 51st (Highland Division) memorial. Leaving the high ground, which marks the *Steinbruch Stellung* (Quarry Position) over your left shoulder, continue down the road. Note that the farmer is still making use of sections of old narrow-gauge railway line, which once ran along this valley, as more or less indestructible fence posts. Take the next track on the right after about one hundred metres, just before the village limit. **(1)** A German communication trench followed the line of this track immediately on your right, facilitating access to *Leilingmulde* (Leiling Hollow) and the trenches of the First Position as far as *Lücke Weg* (Gap Way). As you move along this track, notice the excellent views down the valley towards Beaucourt and beyond.

In the distance, more or less in a direct line beyond Beaucourt, the red roofs of La Grande Ferme three kilometres away may be seen, with a distinct line of trees to its left running north down the hillside. La Grande Ferme is situated just to the rear of the site of the *Schwaben Redoubt* and the trees mark the line of the *Hansa Stellung* (Hanseatic Position), which played an important role in the events of 1st July in that area. This view becomes ever more prominent as you proceed along the track. After about 400 metres the track takes you past the eastern end of *Leiling Schlucht* (Y Ravine), becomes very rough and climbs away fairly steeply towards the present day pylon line past the *Rollbahn* (Runway), which led to the *Leilingstollen* (Leiling Mined Dugout) and was the route of a spur of the narrow gauge railway. Look hard at the chalky escarpment on the far side of Station Road. Dug in along this ridge was a line of machine guns, which covered across to the area of the Newfoundland Memorial and helped to cause huge casualties to the attackers on 1 July 1916. After passing beneath the pylon line and having emerged from the sunken road, stop and look to your left. From here the hole, indicating the exact position of one of these guns, can still be seen towards the right hand end of the escarpment, (binoculars are helpful).

Looking further to the right the very prominent nick of a re-entrant can be seen and followed with the eye as it runs northwards up the slope opposite. This was *Geologen-Graben* (Geologist's Trench = Station Alley) which provided covered access from the south to the redoubt situated on the crest and named the *Grallsburg* after Oberst Grall, commander of Reserve Infantry Regiment 99.

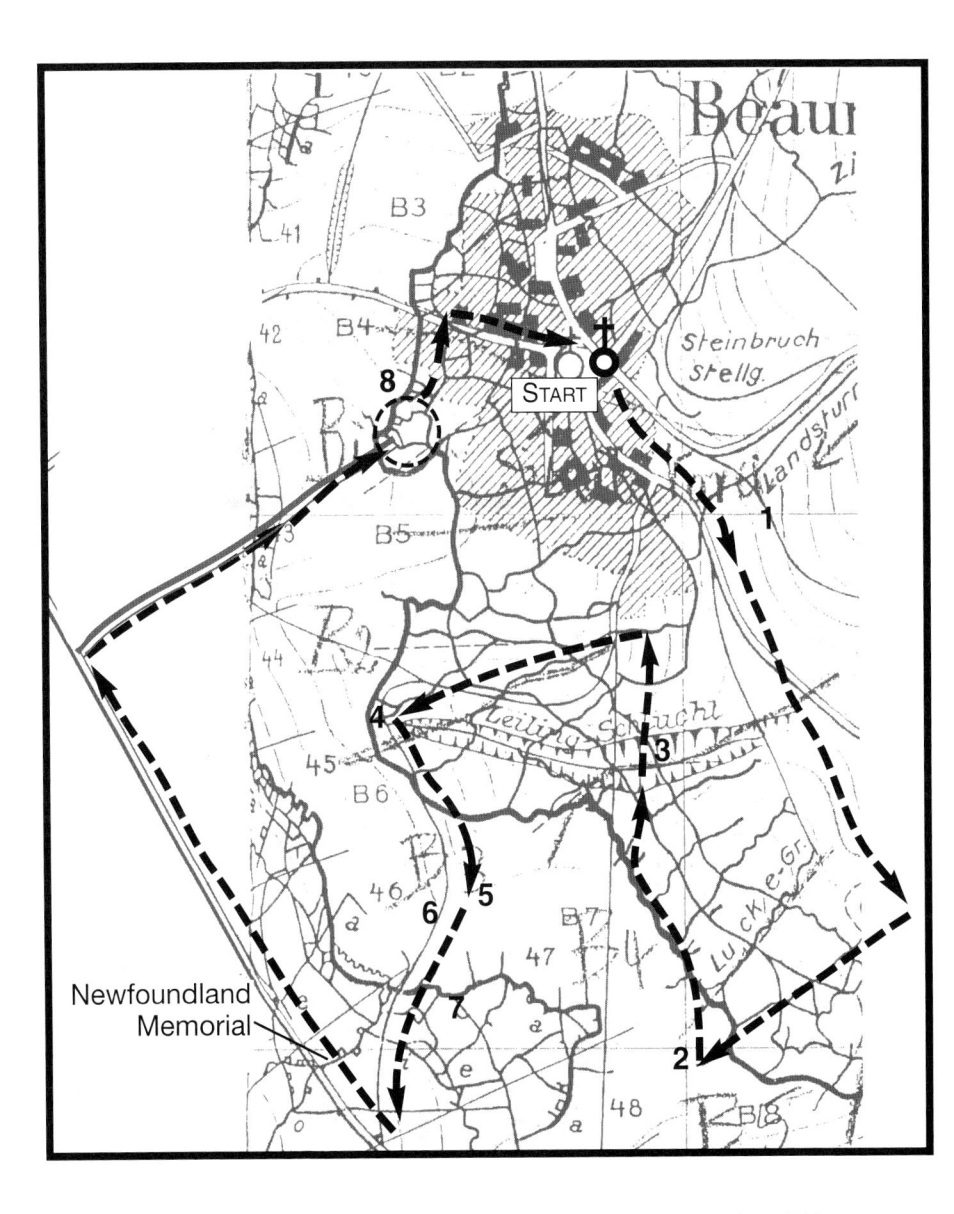

17. Walk 1. Circus, Y Ravine, Newfoundland Memorial and Hawthorn Ridge.

Oberst Friedrich Grall outside Beaucourt Chateau, autumn 1914.

Oberst Friedrich Grall

Oberst Grall was born in Königsberg on 1 March 1859 and brought up in Wesel. In 1879, aged twenty he joined IR 57 as a Fahnenjunker. He was commissioned as a Leutnant in 1880, promoted to Hauptmann in 1894 then, three years later, he was posted to the newly formed IR 159 in Mülheim an der Ruhr. In 1913 he was an Oberstleutnant on the staff of IR 136 in Strasbourg. On the outbreak of war, like many other lieutenant colonels in staff appointments, he was given command of a regiment (Landwehr Regiment 99), but was not in that appointment for very long before the wounding of Oberstleutant Rayle on 21 August 1914 meant that he was appointed commander of RIR 99. He was a highly respected commander who, making light of his comparatively advanced age, was personally involved in the assault on Beaucourt at the head of his leading companies. It could be argued that that was no place for the regimental commander to be, but it was in the nature of the man.

He threw himself fully into command, but the privations of the hard winter of 1914-1915 affected his health. Having been hospitalised twice in 1915, he was transferred to a headquarters staff appointment, but not before the embryonic earthworks on the heights above Beaumont Hamel had been named the Grallsburg after him. He had a busy war, going on to command 6th Guards IR at Verdun in 1916, to spend a period as Commandant of Königsberg and to command IR 403 and 96th Reserve Infantry Brigade on the Dutch border and in the Vosges. He took part in the battle of Armentières in January 1918, then became Inspector of First Army Field Recruit Depot and finally led a large body of men from First Army back into Germany via the Eifel and the Hunsrück after the armistice. After retirement from the army he settled down in Canstatt, near Stuttgart, (which was very appropriate after his close association with 26th Reserve Division) and devoted the remainder of his active life to working for the benefit of those who had been expelled from or left Alsace-Lorraine.

The village war memorial, Station Road, Beaumont Hamel.

A short distance up the re-entrant, very close to where a prominent bushy-topped tree grows, the *Hang Stellung* (Slope Position = Station Trench) contoured away eastwards parallel to the modern road. **Continue along the track into a slight dip.** To your left the torn nature of the ground of the *Cirkus* (Circus) is very evident. A trench, which linked with *Geologen-Graben*, ran down the slope towards the road. Eventually the track curves slightly to the east. At this point it is following the line of the third trench of the first German position. The track can be very indistinct here, so keep well in to the edge of the field. As you reach the crest of high ground, the views over to the Ulster Tower and the Thiepval Memorial are first class and an excellent overview may also be had of the ground around Beaucourt, the Ancre Valley and Saint Pierre Divion. **At a track junction** on the high ground, which at certain times of year may be quite indistinct, **turn sharp right**, heading west directly towards the mass of dark trees which mark the Newfoundland Memorial and crossing the lines of *Kalkweg* (Chalk Way) and *Neue Weg* (New Way), through the full depth of the first position, which was about 400 metres deep at this point.

Turn right (north) at the next road/track junction. **(2)** From this point, looking north northwest past the eastern edge of the Newfoundland Memorial two distinct bushy topped trees can be seen. These indicate the site of Hawthorn Ridge Cemetery No. 1 and further round to the right, a clump of trees marks Hawthorn Crater. Pass beneath the power cables, then **stop** where the broad track narrows and roughens and look to your right. It is interesting to note that at this point the German front line was located on a reverse slope. The entrance to the *Leiling Stollen* was a few metres into the field where the ground drops away. This major mined dugout offered complete protection to a large number of men during the bombardments. Now look to your left and see how the position dominates the ground covered by the Newfoundland Memorial. If you visualise the area minus the trees that surround the Memorial, it is obvious why the defenders moved their

18. Primary and secondary machine gun positions and arcs of fire Beaumont South July 1916. Not all these positions were manned simultaneously, but this still represents formidable firepower. Note, in particular, the gun positions on high ground from Beaumont Hamel to St Pierre Divion. These were the weapons that did most of the damage on 1 July 1916.

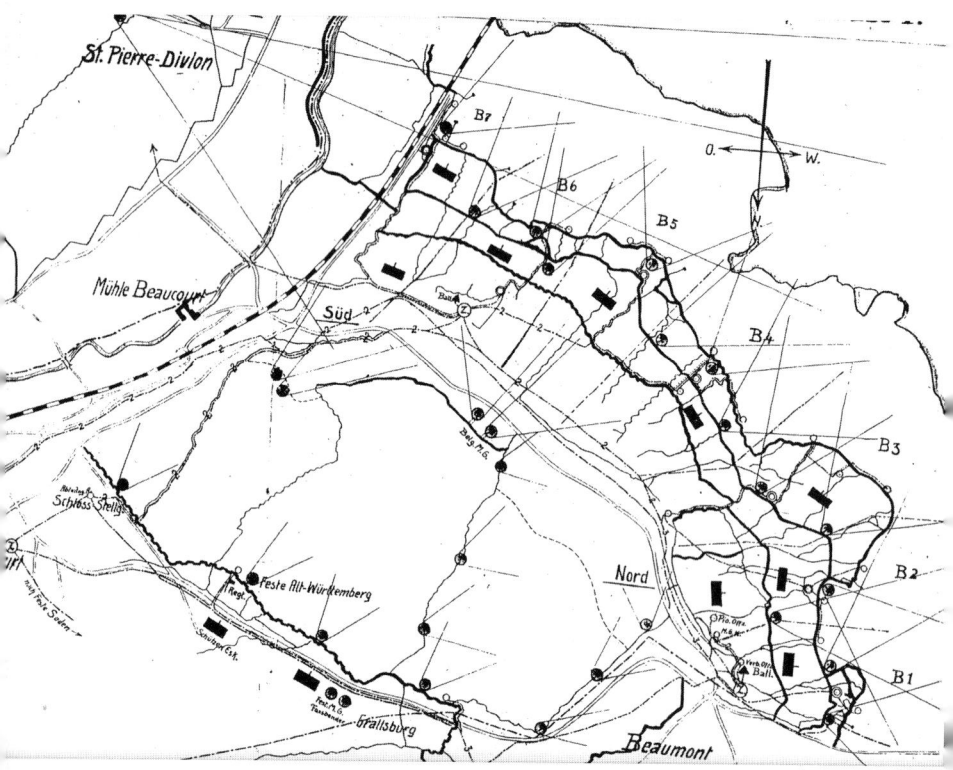

machine guns forward in this area to improve the fields of fire during the morning of 1 July 1916. Now look out above Beaumont Hamel to the high ground of the *Steinbruch Stellung* (Quarry Position) and the *Grallsburg*. All of these places were within easy machine gun range of the Memorial and the defenders had plenty of weapons and ammunition. No wonder that attempts to attack the German lines during fine weather were utterly doomed.

Continue north along the rough track which, as it descends towards Y Ravine, follows the exact line of the old German front line trench, before it swung away west, cutting across the corner of the field to the white concrete posts of the Memorial to pass to the south of the ravine. Stop at the lowest point of the track. This is *Leiling Mulde* (Leiling Hollow). **(3)** This is the point from which the highly successful trench raid of 6/7 April 1916 was launched and recovered. It was full of dugouts of all types. The route the raiders took ran south west for several hundred metres along the eastern side of the Memorial. From this point *Leiling Schlucht* (Y Ravine) runs off to the left. Note that there is no entry to the Memorial from this point, nor is access permitted to Y Ravine.

Carry on up the slope to the next junction, by a minor electricity line and **turn left**. The track follows the line of an old communication trench. Just as it emerges from being slightly sunken and where it bends left towards the entrance to the Newfoundland Memorial, look to your right. This slight knoll **(4)** is the place where a machine gun of Reserve Infantry Regiment 119 was located and was able to cut swathes through the ranks of the British and Newfoundland attackers on 1 July. Enter the Memorial and look down into Y Ravine on your left. The grass-covered mounds in the centre of the ravine are heaps of spoil from a major tunnel, the *Schlucht-Stollen* (Ravine Dugout) which ran westwards from the tip of

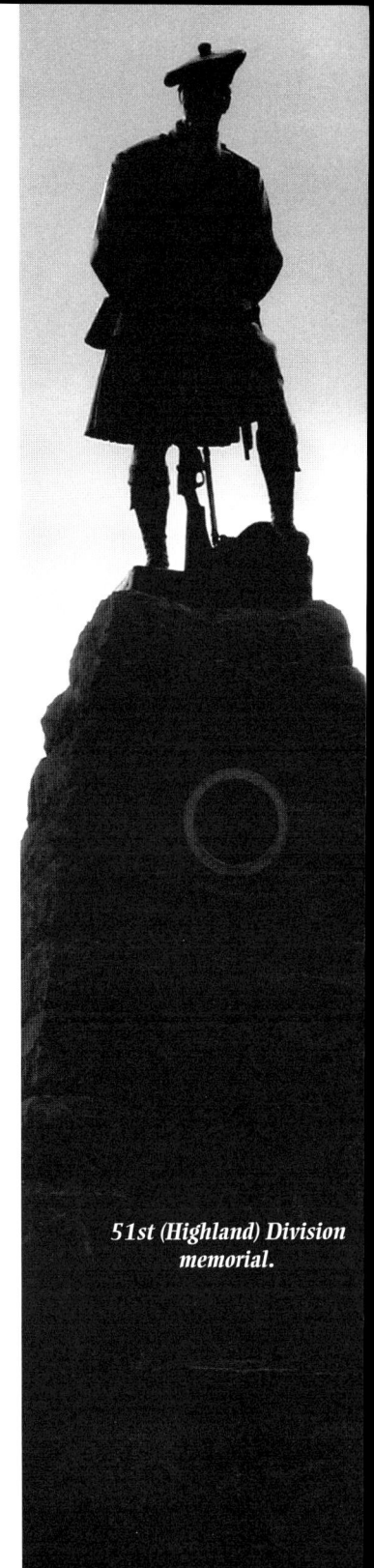

51st (Highland) Division memorial.

Spoil mounds Y Ravine.

the ravine. On your right are various points of subsidence where this tunnel has collapsed over the years. You may wish now to take some time to visit Hawthorn Ridge Number 2 and Hunter's Cemeteries and to examine the 51st (Highland) Division Memorial. The two last were placed exactly on the line of the German front line trench.

Follow the road out of the Memorial, past Y Ravine Cemetery, which is situated in what was No Man's Land, pausing to examine the German front line trench. It is also worth getting down on the ground (whilst respecting the fences) and looking up the slope towards the Caribou to get an idea of the relatively limited view the defenders had in this area. Some writers assert that on 1 July 1916 there was German machine gun fire from the actual parapet of the trench above Y Ravine. This is far from certain. Contemporary maps show exactly where the planned firing points were located. There was one potential weapon position just above the *Schlucht-Stollen*, but it was sited with its arc of fire to the west. A further position was very close to the point where the eastern side of the present day memorial emerges from Y Ravine, but it is not clear that these locations were either the primary gun positions, or that they were actually occupied on 1 July: which would be no surprise. Neither of the places is a particularly good location for an automatic weapon. To be effective, machine guns need to be sited where they have long fields of fire and where from defilade positions they can bring down interlocking enfilade fire in cooperation with weapons to their left and right. No infantryman worth his salt would be so stupid as to site his main defensive weapons where the range is so short and the arcs of fire so limited, or where he could lose his weapons if the first trench was overrun.

At the edge of the Memorial, stop and look east across to the German front line you passed earlier, from where the defenders were able to put down lacerating fire on the 1 July. It is easy to see how good the mutual support was at this point. **Turn right**. **(5)** You are now following the exact line of the 6 April 1916 trench raid as it passed through No Man's Land. As you draw level with the bank where the Danger Tree stands, you are in the area where the final rendezvous for the raid was located. This point was secured by part of the covering force, drawn from 5th Company Reserve Infantry Regiment 119 and comprised twenty four other ranks, led by Reserve Leutnant Burger and Vizefeldwebel Walzer.

Here the attacking force divided into three. The seventeen-strong Group I under Fähnrich Becker stayed on the line of the modern road, whilst Group II commanded by Reserve Leutnant Stenfeld and Group III led by Reserve Leutnant Raiser branched off in two directions to the left in order to ensure that there was a wide spread in the break-in

The German front line, Newfoundland Memorial.

points into Target Area 47. See Map 6. In all the raid went in on a frontage of almost two hundred metres; Group I entering the British lines a short distance to the north of the garden surrounding the Director's house today **(6)** and the other two near advanced saps pushed forward east of the current track between Burlington Arcade and Shaftesbury Avenue. **(7)** Note that the grounds of the Director's house are private property and there is no admittance. Continue to the end of the track where it meets the main road. This point is beyond the British front line and reserve positions.

Turn right and, keeping well into the verge, walk to the northwest past the entrance to the Newfoundland Memorial. There are excellent toilets in the new Visitor Centre at the Memorial, should you need them. If you have not visited the Memorial, this would be a possible time to do so, but it would be necessary to allow an additional one hour for the visit. Guided tours are available, as is an excellent self-guided tour brochure. **Continue along the road to the turn** signposted to Hawthorn Ridge Cemetery No. 1. As you approach the cemetery there are superb long views to the north over Redan Ridge. Passing the cemetery to your right continue along the obvious route to the large clump of trees which mark the site of Hawthorn Crater. **(8)** There is no track which leads directly to the crater, but there are clearly defined field edges, which can be followed, taking care to avoid walking on any crops. This is the site of what the Germans referred to as the northern arm of the *Zange* (Pincers). Although the Allies referred to it as Hawthorn Redoubt, it was not a true redoubt, in that it was never developed for all-round defence as the *Grallsburg* or *Feste Soden* were, but it certainly occupied a dominating position.

In fact up until late spring 1916, when a new trench was dug linking the area of the crater with the northern tip of the Memorial, it was a

The view from Hawthorn Crater to the Sunken Road, Beaumont Hamel.

Hawthorn Crater July 1916.

dangerously isolated salient, which was the object of a failed British raid on 30 April 1916. From the northern tip of the crater the view down to the sunken road by the memorial to 8th Battalion Argyll and Sutherland Highlanders and Beaumont Hamel Cemetery is excellent. It is a sobering thought that on 1 July 1916, almost all the casualties suffered by the Lancashire Fusiliers occurred between the sunken road and the cemetery. It is possible with care to descend into the crater where, if you have a good imagination, you can visualise the two seats of the explosions, but this is not recommended. Apart from the considerable risk of slipping in wet weather and possibly injuring yourself, descents into such places simply accelerate the rate of erosion and contribute to the destruction of the site.

Nevertheless, this is a special place, so take time to walk round as much of it as possible, noting the commanding views and gaining an impression of the dimensions of this enormous crater, which was blown twice – first on 1 July 1916, then again on 13 November. Only about twenty percent of the Germans who were killed on the Somme have known graves and there are no memorials to the missing. But in a real sense this is one of their memorials. Everywhere where you stand you are treading on the mortal remains of a great many men from 9th Company Reserve Infantry Regiment 119 killed on 1 July and a large number from Infantry Regiment 62 who died when the mine was blown for a second time on 13 November. Some are interred many metres down in the remains of their crushed dugouts, others are just below the surface, so tread softly, reflect and as you look down into the crater consider this: Hawthorn Crater is not just a great void; it is a war grave. Pause; and as you watch how the breeze stirs the leaves and branches of the trees which have grown up here, remember. Head back to Beaumont Hamel via the steep and frequently slippery path, taking care to avoid the rusty barbed wire and sharp pickets and return to your car.

Musketen

Conscious of the need to increase firepower in the infantry, a German War Ministry Decree, dated 10 August 1915, directed the raising of two (originally possibly three) *Musketen* battalions. The title Musket, with its echoes of stylised 18th Century warfare, but allegedly adopted as a deception measure, was applied to the

A four-man Musket team, (gunner, loader and two ammunition carriers)

Danish Madsen light machine gun, which slightly resembles the later Bren gun. Each battalion was to be of three companies, each with 176 men and constructed around thirty four-man gun teams, comprising gunner, loader and ammunition carriers. Bearing in mind the need for spare guns, the total quantity available was probably somewhere around 200.

The Madsen, an air-cooled, recoil-operated, light automatic weapon with a twenty five round magazine, was originally developed in 1896 in Denmark by Captain WO Madsen, who was an artillery officer. It was adopted

by the Danish army in 1903 and was exported to Russia, which made extensive use of it in the 1904-1905 Russo-Japanese war. The weapons used to equip the two battalions were part of a shipment from Denmark to Bulgaria, which were diverted by the German army. Some were handed on later to the Austrians and the remainder were delivered to the *Musketen* battalions. Each gun was supplied with 800 rounds in thirty two magazines and 20,000 rounds were available in each battalion as an immediate reserve.

On 10 March 1916 the War Ministry decided to designate the two *Musketen* battalions, 4th and 5th Battalions, Infantry Regiment 117. The reason for this association with one of the regiments from Hessen, which was just coming to the end of its first tour at Verdun at that time, is obscure. Possibly it was another attempt at camouflaging the purpose of these units, which may have then been deployed in the area. Some sources state that *Musketen* companies wore the regimental accoutrements of IR 117 for a while. The regimental history makes no mention of it and in any case the decision was rescinded within a month and 1st and 2nd *Musketen* Battalions were launched as independent units. By the time the Battle of the Somme opened, elements of the 1st *Musketen* Battalion were under command of 26th Reserve Division. The bulk of the weapons appear to have been used in defence of the Thiepval ridge. This is confirmed in numerous contemporary documents. During the final battle for Schwaben Redoubt, for example, no fewer than fifty *Musketen* were involved in its defence. However some were also employed in and around Beaumont Hamel and were involved in the fight for Hawthorn Crater on 1 July 1916.

The Madsen/Musket had a short operational life. Although it fired the standard German 7.92 mm round and had a reasonably fast (450 rounds per minute) cyclic rate, there was a permanent shortage of spares and no way of replacing worn, damaged or destroyed weapons. Furthermore no light magazine-fed weapon could compare with a water-cooled, belt-fed machine gun. They were never designed for sustained firing. By the end of 1916, the Madsens had reached the end of their effective service. Instead, each *Musketen* company was issued with eighteen captured British Lewis guns. The remaining gunners were provided with twenty five round magazines for their Pattern 98 carbines, which were something of a rarity. This improved rates of fire from a maximum of fifteen to twenty five rounds per minute, but these measures simply amounted to a temporary stop gap and the two battalions were amongst the first units to be equipped with the light Maxim 08/15 in early 1917. About a year later, on 22 April 1918, they were re-designated *MG Scharfschützen-abteilungen* (Machine Gun Sharp-shooter Detachments). These units already existed in large numbers, so although the two battalions were allowed to retain their titles, this unique experiment came to an end and *Musketen* faded into a footnote in history.

Walk 2
Redan Ridge, Beaumont North Minefield, *Heidenkopf* Sector
and Feste Soden
This walk can easily take three hours, depending on how much time is spent at each point of interest.

51st(Highland) Division memorial flag pole base, Beaumont Hamel.

Park your car by the church in Beaumont Hamel and take the road towards Auchonvillers. Notice the base of a flagpole on your right. This was presented by the 51st (Highland) Division to the village of Beaumont Hamel on the same day as their memorial was dedicated. It is currently the subject of a restoration appeal; the complete flagpole should be back in place by November 2006. As you leave the final building behind, you are crossing the line of the third trench of the German First Position. **Continue westwards** and pause as you draw level with the southwest corner of the prominent wood on your right. **(1)** You are now standing on the position of the German front line trench. Although the fields of fire from the forward edge of the wood are not especially extensive, small arms fire from this sector had an utterly catastrophic effect at close range on 1 July 1916. Continue to where a track, adjacent to the prominent memorial to 8th Battalion Argyll and Sutherland Highlanders and signposted to Beaumont Hamel British Cemetery, leads north towards a sunken road.

This is a good opportunity to visit the cemetery, should you wish to do so. Once in the sunken road, climb up the bank alongside the sunken road, **(2)** looking back in the direction of the wood beyond Beaumont Hamel cemetery and up towards the site of the mine on Hawthorn Ridge. The German First Position utterly dominates everything here; no wonder that the men of the 29th Division stood no chance whatsoever on the opening day of the battle as they attempted to assault the village of Beaumont Hamel directly. This place evokes the feeling of naked vulnerability of the British attacking infantry more than almost any other point along the Old Front Line. **Follow the sunken road** uphill as it bends gently to the right until, after approximately 400 metres, a track junction is met. **Turn right** along a rough track, which was known to the British as Watling Street. Within a few metres is the entrance to Redan Ridge Cemetery Number 2. This cemetery is located in the former No Man's Land about seventy five metres short of the German front line trench and contains the graves of numerous men who fell on 1 July 1916.

Continue along the track and just where it begins to bend left, you are standing on the location of the German front line. **(3)** Pause and look down hill towards the corner of the wood and over towards

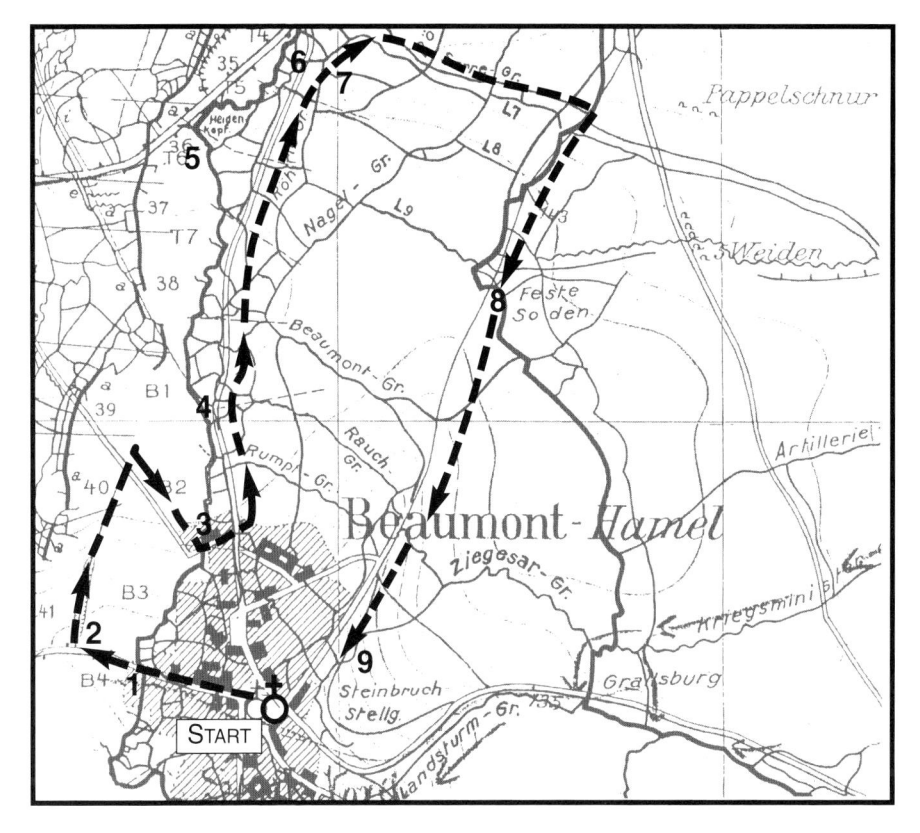

19. Walk 2. Redan Ridge, Minefield, Heidenkopf and Feste Soden.

The remains of the building above the Bergwerk (Mine) in 1915.

Beaumont Hamel military cemetery. Once more, the vulnerability of the attackers is very evident. Continue towards the junction with a metalled road (Frontier Lane). On your right was the area known as the *Bergwerk* (Mine). The defences here were constructed above a former chalk mine, which provided extensive underground accommodation for the trench garrison. A pair of machine guns, which had a devastating effect on the attackers on 1 July 1916, was deployed on either side of this junction facing west. **Turn left** here. Because of the shape of the ground with its convex contours, the layout of the German First Position was quite complicated in this area, but the second trench of the first position ran more or less parallel with and just to the left of the road here. **Continue about 400 metres** to the road track junction and take the left hand fork leading towards Redan Ridge Cemeteries Numbers 1 and 3. **(4)** Although this track is firm and dry in the summer, it gets very muddy and soft after rain. A nearby trench and, by extension, this sub-sector was named *Soden Bogen* after the commander of 26th Reserve Division. The entire area to the left of the track was the site of the Beaumont North Minefield, which extended from a point roughly level with Redan Ridge Cemetery Number 3 to approximately 150 metres northeast of Redan Ridge Cemetery Number 1. In disputing the crest line an enormous amount of mining and counter-mining took place from late 1914 to the summer of 1916.

Until quite recently the torn nature of the ground around Redan Ridge Cemetery Number 1 was very evident, but in the past few years most of the craters have been filled in and the ground largely reclaimed by the farmers. Notice once again what a dominating position this relatively insignificant ridge was. Retrace your steps to the road, noting the excellent views back towards Hawthorn Ridge and the edge of the Newfoundland Memorial, all of which are in easy reach of the numerous machine guns which were deployed up here.

Turn left. The modern road traces a course over what used to be the first and second trenches. Stop after 500 metres opposite the rearward eastern tip of the large Serre Road Number 2 Cemetery. The *Heidenkopf* (Quadrilateral), a rather vulnerable salient, occupied a large section of the forward slope of the field to the right of the cemetery. This area was vigorously disputed during the battles of June 1915. As the Battle of Serre was dying away in mid June 1915, it was decided that additional trenching was required here to occupy the dead ground towards the Serre-Mailly road and it was constructed by the men of Regiment Heiden. The following year it was the scene of extremely severe and bloody fighting on 1 July 1916 when, having previously been evacuated and prepared mines had been blown, it was then occupied by the British army and recaptured late in the day by men of Reserve Infantry Regiment 121.

A number of names of trenches and other features in this area date back to the time of the Battle of Serre. *Nagel-Graben*, for example, was

The crew of a dug in trench mortar. These weapons were generally sited in pairs. See the notation E.M. (Erd-Mörser) on Map 20 on page 122, for the location of a pair which defended the Heidenkopf.

The view of the German front line on the forward edge of the wood in H6. For many of the men of the 1st Battalion, Lancashire Fusiliers, this was their last view on earth on 1 July 1916, though the wood was no more than a collection of torn stumps that day.

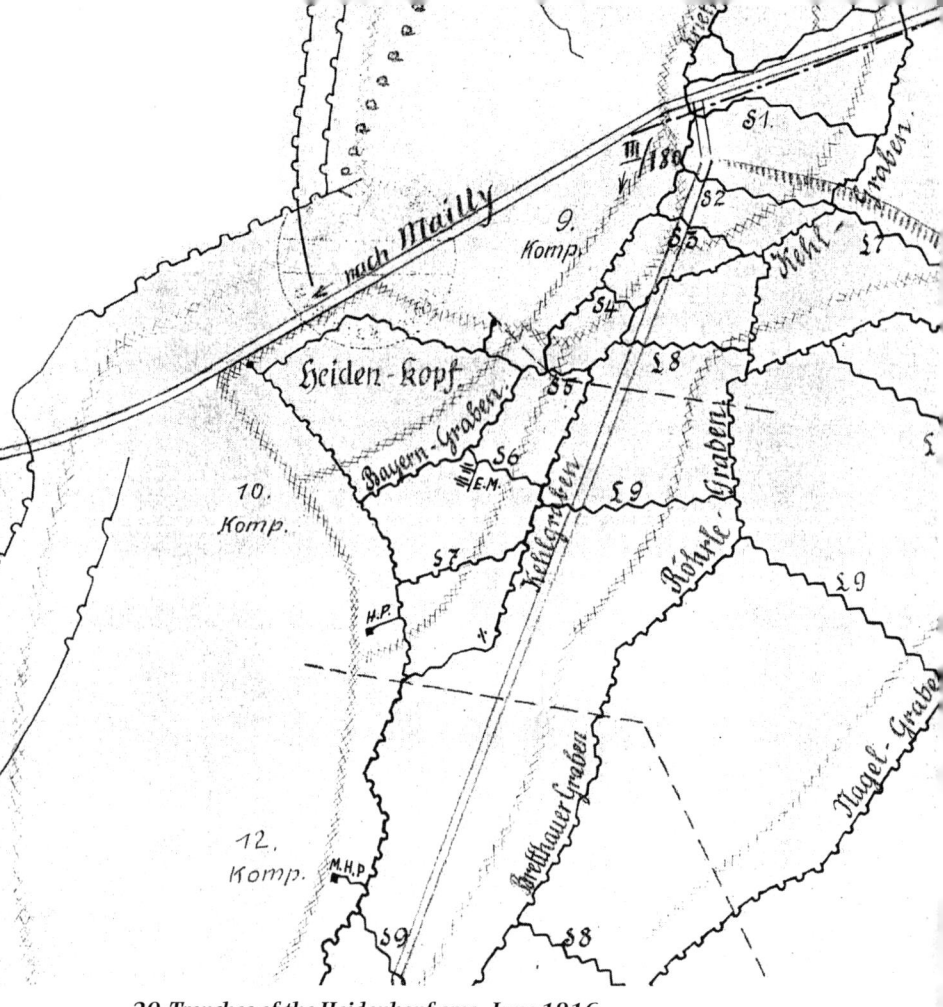

20. Trenches of the Heidenkopf area, June 1916.

named after Hauptmann Nagel, commanding officer 2nd Bn RIR 121, who was killed here on 13 June 1915. The *Heidenkopf*, which could be translated as 'Heathen's Head', was actually named after Major Heiden, who was in command of an ad hoc two-battalion regiment provided by I Bavarian Corps as a reinforcement during the crisis of the Battle of Serre – hence, too, the existence of *Bayerngraben* (Bavaria Trench), which was also christened by this group. These Bavarians may only have spent a few days here, but they certainly left a mark on the geography of the place. A section of the front line of the *Heidenkopf* parallel to and about twenty metres short of the Serre – Mailly road was excavated in October 2003, during the making of a BBC television documentary about Wilfred Owen. **(5)**

As a demonstration of how relatively superficial the original clearance of the battlefield was, removal of less than a half a metre of

Steps leading down to a German dugout in the front line trench of the Heidenkopf exposed during archaeological investigation in October 2003.

The remains of Vizefeldwebel Albert Thielecke, discovered October 2003.

topsoil and detailed investigation of an eight metre stretch of trench by the 'No Man's Land' team of archaeologists sponsored by the National Army Museum, yielded the bodies of three soldiers. Two of them were German who, after painstaking detective work, which involved the Department of Conservation Sciences at University College, London, Ralph Whitehead, an acknowledged American expert on German casualties and detailed work in the German archives, were later identified as Wehrmann Jakob Hönes and Vizefeldwebel Albert Thielecke of RIR 121, who fell during the 1915 battle. The British casualty was an unidentified soldier of the King's Own, possibly from the 1st Battalion, who therefore had probably died on 1 July 1916. Despite all efforts, it was not possible to identify him, but he was buried with full military honours provided by a party from the King's Own Royal Border Regiment in Serre Road Cemetery Number 2 on 24 April 2004. Hönes and Thielecke were buried at Labry German Cemetery,

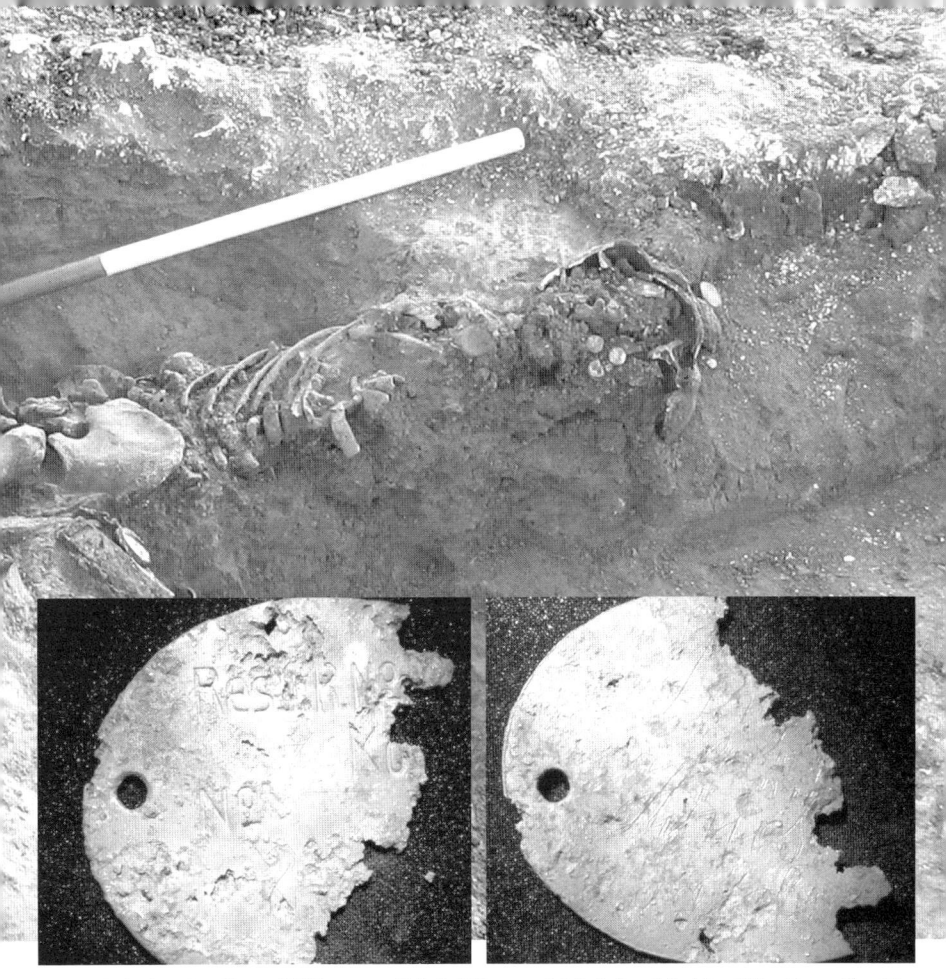

Corroded identity disc of Wehrmann Jakob Hönes, which led to his identification after his discovery in October 2003.
Wehrmann Jakob Hönes and men of 7th Company RIR 121. Hönes is lying front left.

east of Verdun on 26 August 2004. Originally laid out in 1915, this small cemetery has been used for all interments of German soldiers discovered in France since 1989. Thielecke was not conclusively identified (from information found on his documents) until February 2005, but fourteen of Hönes' descendents were present and military honours were provided by a party from a Bundeswehr Signals Unit which was in the area at the time.

Despite its relative vulnerability, it is easy to see why the *Heidenkopf* was constructed. From this point there is a large area of dead ground near the main road, which would otherwise have been invisible to the defenders. Continue along the road, which here marks the line of Kehlgraben, to the main road opposite Serre Road Cemetery Number 1. Turn left and climb the steps to the French memorial chapel. **(6)** On the left by the entry porch is a most rare and unusual sight: a German memorial plaque placed there, presumably in the context of a battlefield pilgrimage, by German veterans in May 1964. In translation the plaque reads, 'In faithful memory of our comrades who fell at Serre. BRIR 1'.

Memorial plaque placed by battlefield pilgrims of Bavarian RIR 1 during a visit in May 1964.

The regiment involved was Bavarian Reserve Infantry Regiment 1, whose individual battalions were stationed here in a reinforcement role with the 33rd Infantry Division from 3 – 17 January 1917. The 33rd was holding a line from south of Serre to the Ancre. The weather was vile and the conditions atrocious. The whole area was one great swamp, made worse by heavy rain on 16 December 1916 and continuing bad weather which never let up for the entire period of their tour. The regiment stated later that even during the worst of the conditions in Flanders in late 1917, there was always some firm ground somewhere, but that did not apply here. It considered Serre to be the bleakest and most dismal place the regiment served in throughout the entire war. The front line had almost disappeared, surviving dugouts were unevenly distributed and there were great gaps in the front line. The terrain was so cut up that soldiers (even an entire company on one occasion) were always getting lost. It was very difficult to move by day and the situation at night was beyond description. All attempts to get trench stores forward failed. The parties either got lost completely or stumbled around until they were utterly exhausted and had to abandon what they were carrying. No hot food could be brought up. Men lost their boots, their weapons and equipment in the mud and some drowned in it. They were under constant large calibre artillery fire. Sentries were frequently

Funeral at Serre Road Cemetery Number 2 of an unknown soldier of the King's Own, killed at the Heidenkopf 1 July 1916, whose remains were discovered in October 2003.

Funeral of Hönes and Thielecke at Labry German Cemetery, 26 August 2004.

View across the rear of Serre Road Number 2 Cemetery and the site of the Heidenkopf to the French Memorial Chapel.

buried alive.

During one two day period, thirteen dugouts in the area of the 2nd Battalion, which was grouped with Infantry Regiment 98, were destroyed, so the garrison had to huddle tightly packed into the seven which remained and battle constantly to keep the entrances clear. This led to the worst single incident of the war for the regiment. Accurate shell fire collapsed the two entrances to a large dug out which housed most of 8th Company. The nearest sections responded to cries for help, but they were spotted and prevented by shrapnel fire from carrying out rescue work that day. They then spent the whole of the following night in the churned up area trying to locate the entrances, but without success. As dawn broke they found that the entire area had been reduced to one great swamp of liquid mud. There was still no trace of the entrances and they had to abandon two officers and forty eight men, some of whom were their most experienced and trusted comrades, to a hideous death, trapped underground and drowned by the ingress of mud.

The regiment was never subject to a major attack, but was ground down by the terrible conditions and constant artillery fire. Large numbers were killed, wounded or evacuated ill. The regiment said later that this awful tour finally finished off the hard core of officers and men who had fought and survived the main battle the previous year. No wonder they decided to place their plaque here. So this modest little memorial, frequently overlooked, has quite a tale to tell. This is a place to pause and, in a moment of personal reflection, remember all who met a dreadful end in the squalid conditions of that winter long ago.

If the weather is dry, return to the junction opposite Serre Road Number 1 Cemetery, turn right, then almost immediately fork left following the curving edge of a rough hedge of trees just south of east.

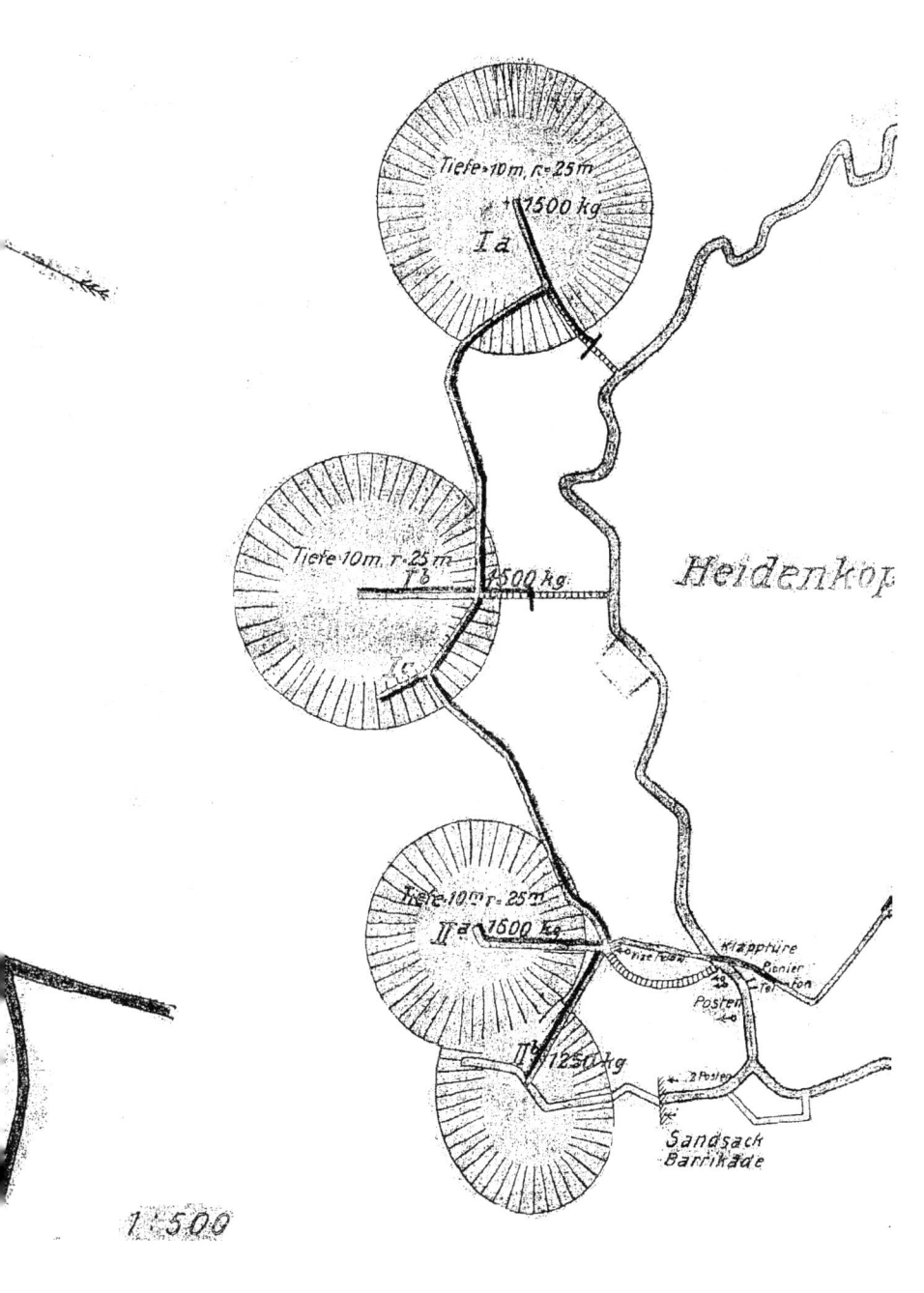

21. Heidenkopf mine craters, blown 1 July 1916.

The site of Feste Soden, looking to the east of Serre.

Men of IR 180 during a quiet moment at Feste Soden during spring 1916.

Opposite: 22. Trench complex Serre – Feste Soden summer 1916.

Feste Soden Summer 1916.

(7) This used to be a field track, but it has been ploughed up. Nevertheless it is possible to follow the field division, which corresponds with the line of the *Serre Graben,* for a few hundred metres to an obvious hedgerow and a cross tracks. Turn right and head uphill south southeast in the direction of Munich Trench and Waggon Road cemeteries.

N.B. In anything but dry weather, after you have visited the chapel continue along the D 919 to Serre. Just after the sign for the village, turn right by a small wayside Calvary. The road bears round to the right and, after about 350 metres, you should turn right up a rough track by a semi-derelict corrugated iron shed. This will lead you to the cross tracks mentioned above. If you use this route, you will have to allow an extra fifteen to twenty minutes for the walk.

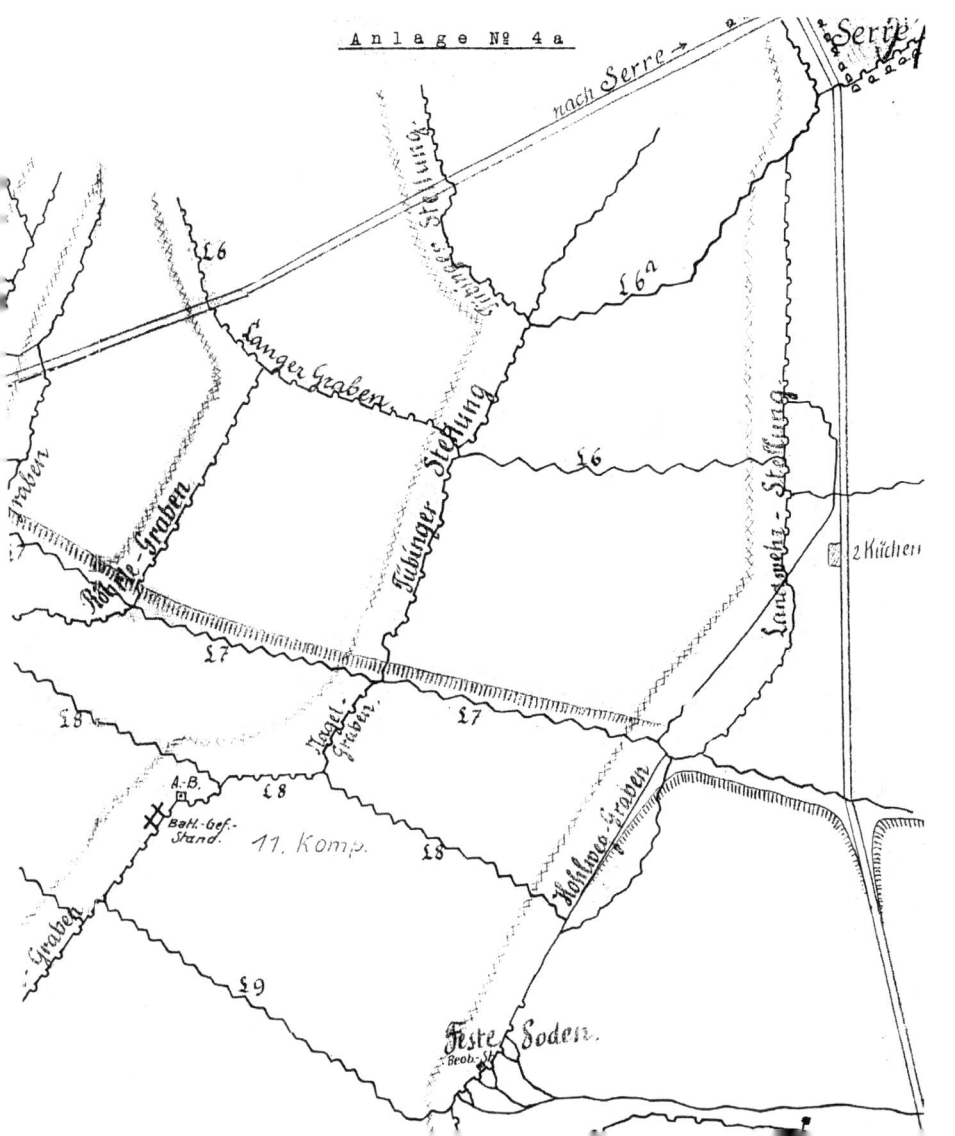

On your left as you walk up the rise was located one of the key parts of the Intermediate Position, which was developed from the third trench of the First Position by the German army during a period of concentrated digging in 1915 and early 1916. This particular section had proved its tactical worth during the Battle of Serre, when it was used as a forward holding area for reserves. Once constructed, it was called *Feste Soden* (Soden Redoubt) **(8)**, having been named, like the *Soden Bogen* one kilometre to the west, after Generalleutnant Freiherr von Soden, divisional commander of 26th Reserve Division. As you approach the first of the cemeteries, the track actually follows the forward edge of the redoubt.

About twenty metres before the turn off to Munich Trench Cemetery, *Kupferschmied Gasse* (Coppersmith Alley), which was where a major communication trench running forward westwards towards *Nagel-Graben*, met the southwest tip of *Feste Soden*. Pause and look in a westerly direction. It is noteworthy that this redoubt was situated in a distinct reverse slope position to an enemy attacking via the *Heidenkopf*, but the views – and hence the fields of fire for its machine guns towards Serre – are spectacular. It should also be stressed that the fields of fire towards the *Heidenkopf* are at least 200 metres, which is more than acceptable from an infantry point of view. From this point *Pappelschnur* (Ten Tree Alley) and its cemetery and *Serre Wäldchen* (Pendant Copse) can be made out clearly. Despite heavy fighting during the November battles, when the area was being held first by IR 23 then by units of 2nd Guards Reserve Division, this particular field fortification was never captured. If you have time, call in at the two cemeteries here. Most of the burials date from late 1916. There are also a few from early 1917 and, because of their isolated locations, they are not much visited.

From here the intermediate position ran due south for one kilometre to the *Grallsburg* feature. Continue along the track towards Beaumont Hamel, crossing the line of a whole succession of communications trenches, which ran down the reverse slope of Redan Ridge towards the sunken road leading back to Beaumont Hamel. After Waggon Road Cemetery a field track meets the road from the right. Just beyond it, where the road becomes sunken, Beaumont-Graben joined. This was followed by *Küchengraben* (Kitchen Trench), *Rauchgraben* (Smoke Trench) and, just before a metalled road to the right, *Rumpfgraben* (Rumpf has various meanings in German: carcass and fuselage amongst them; but it is also a surname, so it is probable that this trench was named after an individual). **(9)** Finally, just as you approach the village, the high ground on your left leads up to the *Steinbruch Stellung* (Quarry Position), where several of the machine guns which caused such heavy casualties to the British attackers on 1 July 1916 were located.

Car Tour of the Rear Area

Summary
Church Beaumont Hamel-Station Road-Beaucourt Station-Beaucourt-Miraumont-Achiet le Petit-Bucquoy – Puisieux-Serre-Beaucourt Redoubt-Beaumont Hamel.

This tour, which can easily take over three hours to complete at a reasonable pace, begins at the church in Beaumont Hamel. Drive down towards Beaucourt along Station Road (D 163 E). Once you exit the village look left to locate a rough, low chalk escarpment. Pause at the far end of this. **(1)** Two thirds of the way up the bank is a hole going back into the chalk. A major tunnel, whose construction was overseen by Hauptmann Leiling of RIR 99, ran along under this escarpment and

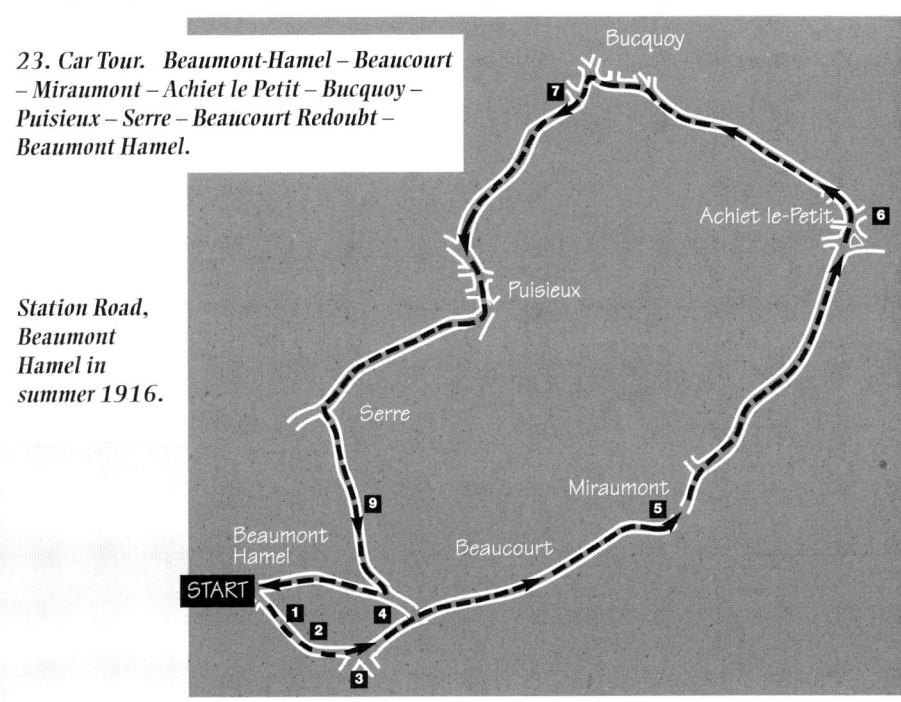

23. Car Tour. Beaumont-Hamel – Beaucourt – Miraumont – Achiet le Petit – Bucquoy – Puisieux – Serre – Beaucourt Redoubt – Beaumont Hamel.

Station Road, Beaumont Hamel in summer 1916.

subsequent hillside towards the station, providing a covered approach route for the troops heading to and from Beaumont Hamel. This is the site of one of the line of eight machine guns spaced out along this road, which had arcs of fire across the present day road and over *Ellrichshausen-Graben*, which ran along roughly parallel with the road through the obviously torn ground behind the German First Position. The more energetic may wish to scramble carefully up the loose rock to the hole. It is not possible to enter it, but the view enjoyed by the gunner can be seen if you lie on your back, with your head level with

Machine Gun position Station Road.

Kolonie, looking for all the world like a navvies' encampment, June 1916.

the hole. From this point the gunner could cover the entire reverse slope behind the First Position with ease and also a large part of the area of the Newfoundland Memorial. In 1916 a narrow gauge railway, which was used to transport ammunition and supplies forward to Beaumont Hamel from Irles and Miraumont, ran along the valley bottom, parallel to the modern road. A spur from it ran up to the *Leiling Stollen* in Sub-Sector B4 almost directly opposite where you are now.

As you proceed to the road junction notice a very prominent re-entrant running away to your left **(2)** and an area of rough ground on the far side of the road. The re-entrant is the precise line of *Geologen-Graben* (Geologist's Trench = Station Alley) which zig-zagged away up the hillside towards the fortification known as the *Grallsburg*. The rough area opposite was known as the *Cirkus* (Circus) and the obvious steep embankment to its south was the *Kolonie* (Colony), where for many months there was a line of dugout billets which provided shelter for the troops in the forward area. The photograph of the *Kolonie* only tells half the story. The semi-dugouts, which resemble a navvies' encampment, disguise the fact that behind them lay deeply mined dugouts and tunnels. When Beaumont Hamel finally fell on 13 November 1916, troops from the 63rd (Royal Naval) Division, outflanking the *Kolonie* from the east, were the men who began the crumbling process which caused the entire First Position to fall.

Carry on to the junction with the main road. You will notice that to the right, diagonally across from the road junction, there is a café which has been established in the old station building by Philippe Feret, who also arranges helicopter rides above the battlefields (Tel: 03 22 74 67 32 www.ensomme.net). **(3)** Philippe is a great enthusiast for

Beaucourt Station in autumn 1916.

Royal Naval Division monument.

the history of the battles. As well as offering a range of drinks and light snacks, he is also in the process of compiling information, artefacts and displays in memory of the 63rd (Royal Naval) Division, which captured the area in November 1916.

Turn left along the D50 (signposted Miraumont) towards Beaucourt. After about 750 metres, stop by the monument to the Royal Naval Division and look to your left. Parking is not easy along this busy road, so keep well in to the side on the right and use your hazard warning lights. **(4)** The minor road up past the memorial marks the line of the *Schloss-Stellung* (Chateau Position), which was defended by men of Reserve Infantry Regiment 55 during the assault on Beaucourt on 13 November 1916 until, outflanked, they had to withdraw up towards *Feste Alt-Württemberg* (Beaucourt Redoubt), which was located 500 metres up the slope in and around Point 123 (121 in 1916). This redoubt was named by the men of RIR 121 who originally dug it; their regimental sub-title being *Alt-Württemberg* (Old Württemberg). If you scramble with care up the bank to the fence by the memorial it is

The Artillerie Mulde (Artillery Hollow) Beaucourt

possible to see that the fields of fire back down towards the station were quite extensive.

Carry on through Beaucourt and, as you exit the village, the road curves to the right and a deep re-entrant, called Vallée Guillotte on the modern map, runs away northwards on your left. This was the

Narrow gauge railway construction, Artillerie Mulde, spring 1916.

26th Reserve Division reading room Miraumont. The concert pianist Nowowiejski is seated second from left, with his elbow on a table.

Artilleriemulde Beaucourt (Artillery Hollow, Beaucourt). Early in the war it was quite common for each regiment to establish its own cemetery. That of Reserve Field Artillery Regiment 26 was established close to this point in autumn 1914. There is room to park beyond the right hand curve if you wish to look more closely at the valley and to see what an excellent position it offered to the guns.

Carry on in the direction of Miraumont, location for some months in 1914-15 of Divisional Headquarters of 26th Reserve Division before it re-located to Biefvillers. Also based here were reserve units out of the line, a casualty clearing station and various administrative elements, including a de-lousing facility. It was also the location of the divisional memorial and war cemetery, which were dedicated as early as **Miraumont in July 1916.**

December 1914 and visited by the King of Württemberg in 1915 and 1916. The modern church is a replacement for the original one, which was located adjacent to the communal cemetery. During the Great War, church services for the many devout Roman Catholics of the 26th Reserve Division were a regular feature here and concerts were also held in the church. As well as its regimental bands, the 26th Reserve Division also numbered several professional musicians in its ranks. One of its reinforcing reservists was a well-known classical concert pianist called Nowowiejski, who starred in these concerts. He was obviously too

Vizefeldwebel Böcker 6th Company RIR 119 is shown here in Beaumont Hamel and together with men who made up his usual patrol, forward of Hamel near the enemy lines in 1915. In civilian life he was a professional opera singer, who often sang in concerts given in the church at Miraumont. He was a fine soldier and a daring patrol commander, who also went out alone on occasions. Caught in an ambush on a solo mission on 9 April 1916, his comrades rushed out in No Man's Land and recovered him, mortally wounded, into a forward trench where he died. He is believed to have been buried in the RIR 119 cemetery in Beaumont Hamel, which was wiped off the face of the earth during the bombardment. Böcker, like so many others buried there, has no known grave.

valuable to morale to be risked in the forward areas, so he was put in charge of the divisional reading room in Miraumont. Vizefeldwebel Böcker, a platoon commander with 6th Company RIR 119, who was a professional opera singer in civilian life also featured in these concerts, but he was also a noted leader of patrols so, until his death on 9 April 1916, he generally spent his time in the front line.

To find the cemetery, drive to where the **D107 turns off towards Courcelette** and turn left up the Rue du Cimetière. **(5)** There is limited parking space for cars outside the cemetery, but not for coaches. It is well worth visiting this cemetery, which as well as being the site for the principal cemetery and memorial to the 26th Reserve Division during the war, also houses in a small plot at the far end several significant burials from the period before the main battle. On numerous occasions the German army recovered the bodies of men who died as a result of trench raids or patrol clashes in No Man's Land, or brought in wounded men who later succumbed to their injuries.

Amongst those buried here are several men of the Royal Irish Rifles killed in 1915 and Lance Corporal AE Fry, Private H Lloyd and Private J Tordoff of the South Wales Borderers, all of whom died during the abortive retaliatory raid against Hawthorn Ridge on 30 April 1916. Also buried here are three senior members of the Dorsetshire Regiment: Captain WB Algeo MC, Lieutenant HGM Mansell-Pleydell, the intelligence officer and Sergeant W Goodwillie, the pioneer sergeant. These three were killed on 17 May 1916 as a result of carelessly clashing with a German patrol only ten days after there had been a German raid against Hammerhead Sap, near the eastern tip of Thiepval Wood. The circumstances of this incident are described in detail in the **Battleground Europe** guide *Thiepval* by Michael Stedman. According to the history of RIR 99, they were buried with full military honours in the presence of the regimental commander, Major

The photographs show successively the visit of the King of Württemberg to Miraumont on 13 April 1915, a divisional service of remembrance around the 26th Reserve Division Memorial on All Souls Day (2 November) 1915, Miraumont New Cemetery situated in the field below the current Communal Cemetery and the wreckage of Miraumont Church and the German cemeteries after the Battle of the Somme. 26th Reserve Division was swift to establish a divisional cemetery around the church in Miraumont and a stone obelisk was unveiled in December 1914 as a memorial to the fallen. During the next few months, all available space was used up, so the field below and to the right of the current Communal Cemetery was annexed in 1915 and dedicated for use as a war cemetery. Eventually a very large number of German soldiers were interred here, together with British soldiers who had been killed during raids and patrols in No Man's Land. The fighting on the Somme left the site very badly damaged by the end of the war. Substantial numbers of British casualties were removed from here to be concentrated elsewhere, but a few remain to this day. There is no trace of the German memorials or any of the casualties who were buried here – anywhere. There are rumours about their fate. It has been alleged, for example, that their bodies were unceremoniously removed and burned elsewhere, but the only certainty is that they had known graves and now they do not. Those who knew, or know, for sure, what happened to them, have either passed on, or are keeping their counsel.

Hans von Fabeck and the other officers of the regimental staff. Apparently this took place in Courcelette so, if true, why they were moved to their present resting place is something of a mystery.

Leave Miraumont on the D50 heading towards Achiet le Petit. About 100 metres after you enter the village a black and white sign placed by the Volksbund Deutsche Kriegsgräberfürsorge indicates a

Miraumont Church and German Cemetery before being wrecked and after the battle of the Somme.

Volksbund sign to Achiet le Petit Cemetery.

right turn. The next sign is quite difficult to see, being set back into a hedge. Turn left here, along the Rue du Cimetière, drive past the communal cemetery, which contains the graves of the members of an RAF bomber crew from the Second World War who were killed on 11 April 1944, and stop outside the attractively landscaped German cemetery. **(6)** With a total of 1,314 burials this cemetery is one of the smaller of its type. It was originally begun, probably in extension of the communal cemetery, in 1914 to gather together scattered graves from what the German army called the First Battle of the Somme, i.e. the battles from September to December 1914, but most of the burials date from the main Battle of the Somme from July – November 1916. Post-war, in 1924, the French military authorities concentrated a further 300 graves from twelve surrounding communes here. Amongst the burials here are Musketier Wihelm Braun IR 413, killed 17 October 1916 (Grave 911); Gefreiter Emil Rieth 4th Company IR 413, killed 15 October 1916 (Grave 1204); Musketier Adolf Rücker 2nd Company IR 413, killed 23 October 1916 (Grave 931) and Unteroffizier Friedrich Roff, 6th Company IR 413, killed on 23 October 1916 (Grave 34). All four fell at Serre. Lying here also is Gefreiter Herbert Schön, 2nd Machine Gun Company RIR 99, killed at Hébuterne 14 September 1916 (Grave 390) and the cemetery probably contains other men of 26th Reserve Division.

The current cemetery marker Achiet le Petit.

This is overwhelmingly a cemetery of junior ranks, with a few subaltern officers scattered amongst them. It is small enough for the visitor to spend a few moments walking up and down all the rows of graves. There are two Jewish graves here. The two lines of Hebrew inscription on them translate as 'Here lies buried' and 'May his soul be intertwined in the circle of the living'. The trees and the hedge of holly and hornbeam were allegedly planted as early as 1927, though that claim does not seem to correspond to the description below of the condition of the cemetery in 1929. Metal crosses were substituted finally for the original wooden crosses as late as 1978 as part of a major action at that time by one of the Youth Camps established for

Achiet le Petit Cemetery June 1916.

the purpose by the *Volksbund Deutsche Kriegsgräberfürsorge* e.V. the German War Graves charity. In grave 785 lies Seesoldat (Marine) Paul Hausen of the Marine Infantry Brigade, which fought so hard against the Canadians in the battles for Regina Trench near Courcelette in October 1916. He may have been one of the very few of the Brigade fallen who were visited after the war, because comrades from Marine Infantry Regiment 1 are known to have visited this site on a battlefield pilgrimage in May 1929 looking for the graves of the men of the Brigade. Writing later, Theodore Kinder said of the experience,

We criss-crossed the area around Cambrai, Bapaume and Albert where the division (i.e. The Marine Infantry Brigade), was deployed during 1916 and 1918 and where we had had to leave many hundreds of the fallen behind. Only in three places did we come across

Headstone of Musketier Moritz Faber, who was Jewish and was killed on 1 July 1916.

144

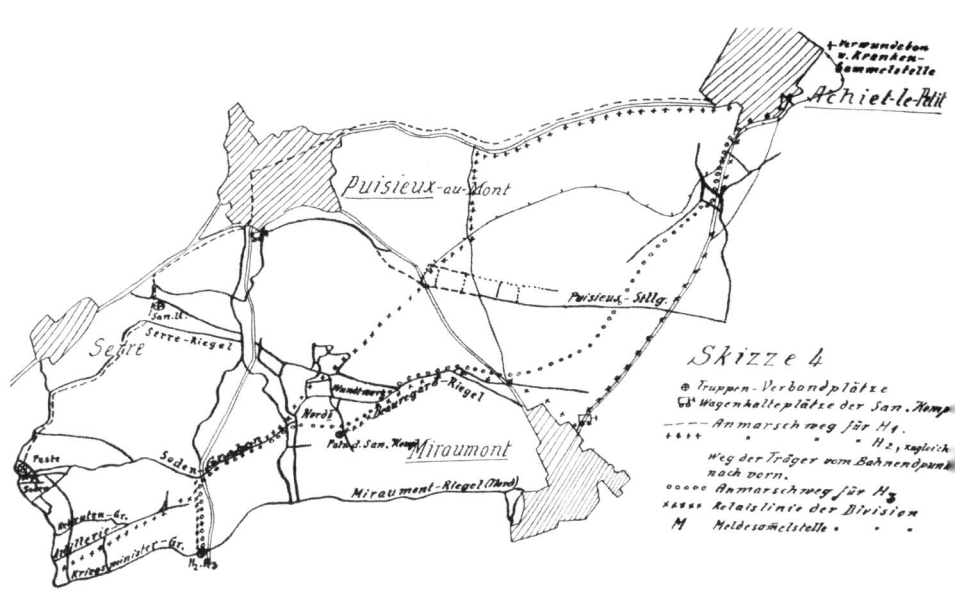

24. German Lines and route map Serre – Miraumont area winter 1916/17.

German graves and in only two of those did we find places where our regimental comrades lay buried. Where was the last resting place of the many others? This unanswered question made us all sad. How many of our comrades had simply been ploughed into the ground when the battlefields were being cleared?

And what a state the cemeteries containing the heroic German dead were in!! For example, after questioning many of the locals and after going wrong on numerous occasions, we found ourselves near Achiet le Petit, where a German cemetery,

Crosses of Unteroffizier Friedrich Ruoff and Musketier Adolf Rücker of 6th and 2nd Companies IR 413 respectively. They were both killed at Serre.

containing about 1,200 of the fallen, lies hidden away. Just as in Belgium, the cemetery was surrounded with barbed wire. The rows of graves were marked by crosses leaning at all angles, with their inscriptions partly or totally unreadable. Fifty crosses lay in a jumbled heap in one corner. Where was the resting place of the dear comrades where these crosses had once stood?*

Kinder went on to contrast this situation with that of the Allied dead, who were increasingly lying in permanent cemeteries by that time and he remarked that the party returned home determined to do all in their power to improve the situation.

Retrace your steps to the main road. **Turn right and then left** onto the **D 8 towards Bucquoy**. At the crossroads in the centre of Bucquoy **turn left on the D919 signposted to Puisieux.** Once clear of Bucquoy, Queen's Cemetery, named for twenty three members of that regiment who fell on 14 March 1917, appears on the right and you may wish to stop and pay your respects. **(7)** Of the 700 graves here, the majority were concentrated after the war. It is interestingly to note that quite a large number were removed from German cemeteries in and around Miraumont. It is immaculately kept and deserves to be better known. **Continue along the D919 through Puisieux** following signs to Albert and Mailly Maillet and carry on towards Serre. Notice as you drive through Serre that you are following the crest line, whose possession was so vital to the German army during the battles of 1915 and 1916 and that from time to time you can see the tops of the trees in the wood that has grown up from Mark, Luke and John Copses and which marks the start line of the abortive attack by the British 31st Division on 1 July 1916.

On your left, just before you leave Serre, there is a small wayside

Barricades providing cover from view along the Puisieux-SerreRoad May 1916.

Calvary at Serre August 1916.

Calvary, where you should **turn left onto a minor, but all-weather, metalled road,** with a 10-Ton weight limit, which heads south across the fields. Shortly after you set off along this road you will notice that excellent views open up down towards the Thiepval Ridge and over to the Newfoundland Memorial. After about one kilometre the very rough track leading to the isolated Ten Tree Alley Cemetery is on your left and you may wish to visit it. **(8) Once you pass under the pylon line on Hill 128 pull up. (9)** This hill is a first class grandstand, offering views over the Thiepval Ridge with its Memorial to the Missing and the Ulster Tower and, further to the left, the red roofs of La Grande Ferme, which mark the rear of the Schwaben Redoubt and a prominent line of trees which run along the line of the *Hansa Stellung* (Hanseatic Position). **Continue to Point 123 and take an acute turn to the right.** This would be extremely difficult, if not impossible, for a coach. The road climbs gently at this point which was another important area for the defence. It was christened *Feste Alt Württemberg* (Beaucourt Redoubt) by the men of RIR 121 who dug it and it commands wide views in all directions. Look hard in the direction of the Newfoundland Memorial. It is easy to see how machine guns firing from here could turn any attempt in fine weather to attack down the hill towards or parallel to Y Ravine into a slaughter. **Carry on under the pylons onto Point 135 and stop once more.** This was the *Grallsburg*, a redoubt named after Oberst Grall, commander of Reserve Infantry Regiment 99 at the time it was first constructed. Once again it is obvious that movement in or around the German First Position, especially in the area of the Newfoundland Memorial, was totally exposed to automatic weapons fired from this point. Continue back to Beaumont Hamel, pausing near the turn off to New Munich and Frankfurt Trench Cemeteries. From here, look across to Redan Ridge, where the cemeteries can be seen clearly. The 500 metres which separates the two lines of cemeteries is the history of the battle in this area – a sobering thought on which to end this tour. The road here follows the line of *Landsturm-Graben* (Homeguard Trench), (notice the torn nature of the ground to your left where pasture has roughly re-grown). The final piece of high ground on your right before you drop back into the village is the *Steinbruch Stellung* (Quarry Position), which also offered first class fields of fire to machine guns located on it.

Supplementary Visit: Fricourt German Cemetery

Fricourt German Cemetery lies outside the area covered by this guide, but as the only such cemetery located within the British area of the Battle of the Somme, a visit to it is an indispensable part of any attempt to follow the activities of the German army during the great battles which took place within a few kilometres. It is located on the eastern side of the D147, the Fricourt-Contalmaison road and, like all German cemeteries, is signposted from the centre of the village after which it is named, with the distinctive black and white signs erected by the *Volksbund Deutsche Kriegsgräberfürsorge e.V.*, the charity which cares for all war graves and cemeteries outside the territory of the Federal Republic of Germany. Each of the signs bears the words 'German Soldiers' Cemetery 1914-18' in German and French, together with the name of the cemetery and the distinctive crest, made up of five crosses. The crosses of the crest: three prominent, with their overtones of Golgotha, supported by two 'lesser Calvaries' in the background, are known to the *Volksbund*, which has some 2,000,000 supporters, as 'Signposts for Peace'.

Unlike the Commonwealth War Graves Commission, the *Volksbund* depends mostly on charitable giving. From time to time the German government has made grants to it, but fund raising amongst its supporters remains a crucial source of income. It does achieve a great deal with limited means but, during the past fifteen years, has been concentrating its efforts in Eastern Europe and the territories of the former Soviet Union, in order to restore dignity to long-neglected, desecrated and plundered burial grounds. This leaves little to spare for further enhancements in Western Europe. The sombre overtones of black and green chime with the German approach to remembrance, but the cemeteries, with their large expanses of lawn, are, perhaps, a little starker than originally intended. It is price that has to be paid for ease of maintenance.

Information concerning Manfred von Richthofen outside Fricourt German Cemetery.

Men of the Württemberg Reserve Dragoons in Feste Alt-Württemberg spring 1916.

After the Great War the question of dealing with the war dead posed massive problems for the German people. Total fatal casualties had exceeded 2,000,000 and, such was the administrative confusion of the closing months of the war, that the records were patchy or non-existent, despite the establishment by War Ministry decree on 28 July 1916 of so-called *Gräberverwaltungsoffiziere* (Graves Administration Officers) on the staff of rear area headquarters along the front. Of the countless burial sites along the Western Front, for example, some men lay in carefully constructed and marked cemeteries created by their comrades, others were hastily buried in cemeteries which were lost in the later fighting and enormous numbers just disappeared into shell holes or trenches scattered around the devastated areas. Under Articles 225 and 226 of the Treaty of Versailles it was the responsibility of the Allies and Germany to respect and care for the graves of servicemen in their respective countries. Here in France, making extensive use of the labour of prisoners of war, a start was made soon after the war to consolidate and record the graves of the German fallen, but the effort and attention to detail bore no comparison, for example, with the scrupulously careful work of the Imperial War Graves Commission; it simply was not a priority. Often the French were not very careful over the recording of the bodies of their own fallen, so it is hardly surprising that the German dead merited even less attention.

To take a local example, roughly 320 officers and men from Reserve Infantry Regiment 111, who were responsible for the defence of this sector, were killed in or around Fricourt between 24 June and 2 July 1916 alone. Fricourt was then evacuated and the battle moved on. Nevertheless all their bodies have disappeared without trace. We do not know what happened to them. Not one of them appears to have a known grave – anywhere. If the slightest effort was really being made to record their burials, how could so many men have been completely unidentifiable? Some may have ended up as an unknown in one or other of the mass graves, but that thought can have been of small comfort to their bereaved families, who did not even have the consolation of seeing their names recorded on a memorial to the missing; there are none.

17,027 soldiers lie here, two and a half times as many as are buried in Serre Road Number 2 Cemetery, which is the biggest of the CWGC cemeteries of the Somme, but even this huge number is not the largest such German concentration on the Somme; that dubious honour is held by Vermandovillers, south of the river, with 22,650 and even that number is dwarfed by the 45,000 buried in one cemetery at Neuville St Vaast near Vimy, which contains many men who fell during the Battle of the Somme. Not all German cemeteries in France are so huge, but their size does reflect the reluctance on behalf of France to grant Germany space to bury its dead after the Great War. About 10,000 of the burials at Fricourt date from before or during the main Battle of the Somme, with about 6,000 from the fighting of 1918. 11,970 men are buried in four huge mass graves, known here as *'Gemeinschaftsgräber'* (communal graves, also referred to as *Kamaradengräber*, comrades' graves). 5,331 individuals are commemorated by name; the rest are unknown. Many of the larger German cemeteries contain mass graves. A very large number of smaller cemeteries and scattered burials were concentrated during the 1920s and then again after the Second World War. This made the task of maintaining them easier and more economical for the *Volksbund*, which has always had problems with funding, but created a problem of space. Mass burials were the answer and a name embossed on a bronze plaque was always provided for known individuals.

Probably the most famous (temporary) occupant of a grave here was the fighter pilot Rittmeister Manfred Baron von Richthofen (The Red Baron). Details about him (heavily edited) are provided in three languages on a noticeboard at the entrance to the cemetery. In fact Richthofen was buried four times altogether. On the first occasion he was given full military honours in a burial by the Australians at Bertangles, not that this prevented his grave from being desecrated by local residents later. On the second he was re-interred here in what is now Block 4 Grave 1177 in 1920, but he was not there for very long. Recovered to Germany in 1925, he lay in state in the Gnadenkirche in Berlin, guarded by surviving fighter pilots who held the Pour le Mérite (Blue Max) and his former comrades from his original Uhlan regiment (Nr. 1 'Kaiser Alexander III') and was given a state funeral, led by President Hindenburg in full Field Marshal's uniform, on 20 November 1925. He was then buried in the heroes' plot of the *Invalidenfriedhof* but, at the request of his family, was finally laid to rest in the

Südfriedhof, Wiesbaden, after the Second World War.

Whenever a funeral with honours took place, or during subsequent commemorations here as elsewhere, it was the practice for the poem, *Ich hatt' einen Kamaraden* (I had a comrade) written in 1809 by Ludwig Uhland (1787 – 1862) to be sung or played, frequently on a solo trumpet, to a tune based on a folk melody and written by Friedrich Silcher in 1825. This piece is effectively the equivalent of Last Post and it is still in use today. By coincidence, Uhland was a native of Tübingen in Schwabia, home of many of the men who served in the Württemberg regiments of 26th Reserve Division.

Ich hatt' einen Kameraden,	I had a good old comrade,
Einen bessern findst du nit.	You'd never find his like.
Die Trommel schlug zum Streite,	When drums beat for a fight,
Er ging an meiner Seite,	He was there right by my side,
In gleichem Schritt und Tritt.	And matched me step for step.
Eine Kugel kam geflogen;	A bullet came a-flying;
Gilt es mir oder gilt es dir?	For me, or was it you?
Ihn hat es weggerissen,	It tore him clean away,
Er liegt mir vor den Füssen,	And at my feet he lay,
Als wär's ein Stück von mir.	So part of me fell too.
Will mir die Hand noch reichen,	Stretch out your hand and grasp mine,
Derweil ich eben lad'.	Whilst I re-load my gun.
Kann dir die Hand nicht geben;	I just can't do it – never;
Bleib du im ew'gen Leben,	But may you live for ever,
Mein guter Kamerad!	My good and brave old pal!

Solemn sentiments and a solemn melody, but soldiers are the same the world over, so Uhland soon found himself parodied by the front line soldiers who, in an echo of the ditty 'Hard Crackers Come Again No More', sung by Union Soldiers in the American Civil War to the tune of 'Hard Times Come Again No More' by Stephen Foster, sang *'Ich hatt'*

Original funeral of Major Hermann von Zeppelin at Bertincourt 10 July 1916. Right: Headstone of Major Hermann von Zeppelin after his re-interment in the Waldfriedhof Stuttgart.

mal Marmelade!' (I once had some jam). As the war went on, if they had not laughed at their poor, sparse rations, they would probably have cried.

As is usually the case in German cemeteries, there are comparatively few officers buried at Fricourt. Such was the poor state and uncertain future of German war cemeteries in the post-war period that many families who could afford to do so paid for the repatriation of the remains of their fallen if they were identifiable. One good example of this is Major Hermann von Zeppelin, commanding officer of 2nd Battalion Reserve Infantry Regiment 122, who fell at Mametz on 10 July 1916. Despite the fact that the battle was raging at the time, his body was recovered to Bertincourt, where he was placed in a coffin and buried with full honours, including regimental band and cortège, in the battlefield cemetery there. His grave survived the subsequent battles and his remains were eventually repatriated to Germany and re-interred in Plot B3E, Row 31, Grave 1299 of the military cemetery within the *Waldfriedhof,* Stuttgart, where there is a great concentration of memorials to the old army of Württemberg.

Permanent landscaping, including the installation of the steps and wrought iron gate, along with initial planting of trees and shrubs, began in 1929, but there was a major overhaul from 1977, when the metal crosses were installed and the hedges and shrubs were renewed. As always, it is extremely difficult to link the named graves to particular regiments and actions, but here follows a list of individuals of 26th Reserve Division, mostly drawn from the Stuttgart area, whose graves are worthy of your attention and appropriate to the places you have been visiting. They are arranged in Block and Grave order to make visiting easier. It is entirely possible that where two or more of these men are buried near to one another, the modern cemetery does in fact house a cluster of men who fell near to each other and who were originally buried together elsewhere on the battle field. It is a sobering illustration of the human cost of the Somme to walk the full length of the *Gemeinschaftsgräber* and to pick out names at random on the bronze tablets. Your eye soon tires of the task, long before the seemingly endless list ends: and remember that the unknowns amount to an even longer list. The presence of a name on a particular tablet is no indication of where the individual lies within the mass graves.

INDIVIDUAL GRAVES

Leutnant Kurt Seidel RIR 121, Beaumont Hamel 1 July 1916. Block (B)1 Grave (G)54. Seidel had been an officer with the regiment since August 1914.
Kriegsfreiwilliger Heinrich Alb, 11th Coy RIR 119 Beaumont Hamel 1 July 1916. B1 G152. Alb was a salesman, who was born in Stuttgart 28 January 1896.
Landsturmmann Ludwig Laiflle, 10th Coy RIR 121 Beaumont Hamel 18 September 1916. Laiflle was a vegetable gardener, who was born in Stuttgart-Heslach 28 October 1888. B1 G203
Wehrmann Hermann Kleinfelder, 10th Coy RIR 119 Beaumont Hamel 26 September 1916. Kleinfelder was a baker, born in Dagersheim, Böblingen 19 February 1881. B1 G223
Unteroffizier Georg Engerer, 11th Coy RIR 119, Beaumont Hamel 1 July 1916. Engerer was a tram driver, who was born in Ansbach 18 October 1889. B1 G1155
Landsturmmann Paul Strobel, 8th Coy RIR 119 Beaumont Hamel 19/20 August 1916. Strobel was a cobbler, who was born in Aalen 8 October 1879. B1 G1239
Kriegsfreiwilliger Heinrich Reinwald, 7th Coy RIR 119 Beaumont Hamel 11 June 1916. Reinwald was a mechanic, who was born near Neckarsulm 3 July 1897. B2 G58
Gefreiter Gustav Götsch, 4thCoy RIR 119 Beaumont Hamel 26 June 1916. Götsch was a building technician, who was born in Stuttgart 26 November 31 January 1891. B2 G163
Kriegsfreiwilliger Karl Gerni, 4th Coy IR 180, Serre 18 December 1915. Gerni was in domestic service before the war. He was born in Stuttgart 10 June 1896. B2 G215
Vizefeldwebel Otto Maier, 5th Coy RIR 119 Beaumont Hamel 30 April 1916. Maier was a bank official, who was born in Stuttgart 14 December 1895. B2 G287.
Gefreiter Friedrich Weinmann, 9th Coy RIR 119, Beaumont Hamel 3 October 1915. Weimann was a postal clerk, who was born near Mergentheim on 24 October 1881. B2 G292
Landsturmmann Ferdinand Ehscheid, 11th Coy IR 180 Serre 14 May 1916. Ehscheid was a gilder who was born in Munich 7 February 1879. B2 G332
Kriegsfreiwilliger Rudolf Egner, 11th Coy RIR 119. Beaumont Hamel 1 July 1916. Egner was a tailor's cutter, who was born in Stuttgart-Gaisburg 8 December 1895. B2 G1156
Unteroffizier Emil Brose, 10th Coy RIR 119 Beaumont Hamel 1 July 1916. Brose was a sculptor of wood, who was born in Stuttgart-Botnang 23 June 1881. B2 G1173.
Kriegsfreiwilliger Wilhelm Burrer, Beaumont Hamel 3 September 1916. Burrer was a salesman in civilian life. B2 G1239

Unteroffizier (Offizier Aspirant) Wilhelm Volz, 12th Coy RIR 119 Beaumont Hamel 8 July 1916. Volz was a teacher, who was born in Stuttgart 16 October 1893. B2 G1241

Oberleutnant Anton Mühlbayer, company commander, 9th Coy RIR 119 Hawthorn Ridge Beaumont Hamel 1 July 1916. Mühlbayer had been employed by the Post Office before the war. He was born in Hall 6 November 1881. B3 G306

Gefreiter Johannes Pölitz, 2nd Coy GrenR 123 Guillemont 21 August 1916. Pölitz was a mechanic who was born near Dresden 11 May 1892. B3 G736

Unteroffizier Richard Anstett, 9th Coy RIR 119, Beaumont Hamel 3 September 1916. Anstett was a cashier in a bank. He was born in Stuttgart 12 August 1890. B3 G1155

Leutnant Erich Rapp, 4th Coy RIR 121 Redan Ridge, north of Beaumont Hamel 1 July 1916. Rapp was a student of mechanical engineering, who was born in Ulm 9 October 1894. B4 G101

Gefreiter Christian Märkle, 2nd Coy Pi Bn 13 Mametz/Fricourt 20 June 1915. Märkle was a builder, who was born in Tübingen 5 September 1889. B4 G133

Gefreiter Hugo Lang, 3rd MG Coy RIR 119, Beaumont Hamel 3 September 1916. Lang, a wartime volunteer, was a mechanic, who was born in Horb 5 February 1898. B4 G185

Pionier Gustav Henninger, 1 Res Pi Coy, Pi Bn 13, SE of Mametz 19 December 1914. Henninger was a gardener, who was born in Oberschaffhauen near Freiburg, Baden 26 May 1890. B4 G367

Kanonier Max Vollmar, 4th Bty 26 Res Fd Arty Regt Courcelette 1 July 1916. Vollmar was a salesman, who was born in Stuttgart 9 December 1887. B4 G396

Grenadier Alois May, 1st Coy Gren Regt 119 19 August 1916. (Probably Delville Wood.) May was a tram driver, who was born in Neunheim 24 January 1887. B4 G731

Equivalent Ranks : German – British

GENERALLEUTNANT	Lieutenant General
GENERALMAJOR	Major General
OBERST	Colonel
OBERSTLEUTNANT	Lieutenant Colonel
MAJOR	Major
HAUPTMANN	Captain
RITTMEISTER	Captain (mounted units)
OBERLEUTNANT	Lieutenant
LEUTNANT	Second Lieutenant
FELDWEBELLEUTNANT	Sergeant Major Lieutenant
OFFIZIERSTELLVERTRETER	Officer Deputy (an NCO appointment, not a rank)
FÄHNRICH/FAHNENJUNKER	Officer Cadet
FELDWEBEL	Sergeant Major
VIZEFELDWEBEL	Staff Sergeant
UNTEROFFIZIER	Corporal
GEFREITER	Lance Corporal
INFANTERIST}	Private – Active Unit
MUSKETIER}	Private – Active Unit
GRENADIER}	Private – Active Unit
ERSATZ-RESERVIST}	Private – Never called up for service in peacetime with an active unit, but a man who had completed basic training and further periods of training as a reservist
KRIEGSFREIWILLIGER}	Private – Wartime volunteer
SCHÜTZE}	Private (usually a machine gunner)
WEHRMANN}	Private (reservist)
LANDSTURMMANN}	Private (Home Guard, but from 1915 could be found in all units)
JÄGER}	Private (Light Infantry Units)
PIONIER}	Sapper
KANONIER}	Gunner

Abbreviations

IR	Infantry Regiment
RIR	Reserve Infantry Regiment
RFAR	Reserve Field Artillery Regiment

Organisation of German Forces in the Beaumont Hamel Area

The area covered by this book was the responsibility of 51 Reserve Brigade, which was one of the two brigades of the 26th Reserve Division from Württemberg in southwest Germany. Prior to 1914 there were two main elements within the Imperial German Army: active units and formations, which were reinforced up to war establishment by individual reservists and reserve units and formations which mirrored their active equivalents, were formed through the call up of individual and collective reservists and were commanded by seconded regulars or those who held reserve commissions. By 1916 the organisation was somewhat more complicated due to the raising of additional wartime units and formations and the fact that Landwehr formations held the line in quieter areas, but as far as active and reserve formations are concerned, they had both been fighting for two years and they knew their business. On the outbreak of war reserve formations, which mirrored their active equivalents were mobilised and deployed. This meant that very few reservists were kept back and consequently it was common to come across men from the Landsturm (Homeguard) in front line units within weeks of the commencement of operations.

51 Reserve Brigade comprised two regiments (RIR 119 and RIR 121), each of three battalions. Each battalion was divided into four companies, each company into three platoons and each platoon into two half platoons of about thirty to thirty five men each. The average strength of a battalion in this division at the beginning of the bombardment on 24 June 1916 was between 850 and 900 men, so the area covered by this book was defended by approximately 5,000 infantrymen divided up between the various trenches of the First Position. Means of communication to the flanks and rear were dug deep, doubled or trebled and backed with flare signals, light signals and relays of runners. They worked virtually faultlessly on 1 July 1916.

By June 1916, each regiment had two machine gun companies; each with six guns, for close protection, but the 1st Machine Gun Company of RIR 119 was detached to provide depth fire to the Second Position near Grandcourt. Altogether, the division had access to over ninety machine guns and thirty *Musketen* (Madsen light machine guns), because it had been issued with an additional nine Russian and twelve Belgian machine guns and had been reinforced by Machine Gun Detachment Fasbender with six guns. The breakdown of weapons between the positions north and south of the Ancre is not easy to determine with total precision, but as far as Beaumont Hamel is concerned, it is known that the Steinbruch Stellung (Quarry Position), the Grallsburg, Hang Stellung (Slope Position) and Feste Alt-Württemberg (Beaucourt Redoubt) were festooned with machine guns and that a pair of machine guns near St Pierre Divion were sited to fire in enfilade up as far as the Y Ravine area. Close protection was provided by the reinforced 2nd Machine Gun Company of RIR 119. Rarely in history can such a death trap have been prepared and remained unsuppressed prior to an attack. This massed firepower was backed by a generous allocation of heavy Albrecht mortars and the heavy guns of the reinforced 26 Reserve Field Artillery Brigade.

51 Reserve Brigade may have been heavily outnumbered, but it was a formidable opponent in the summer of 1916.

Selective Index

Achiet le Petit 24, 141, 143, 14
Aisne 19
Albert 19 – 20, 89, 144, 146
Albrecht Mortars 77, 157
Alsace 31 - 32, 35
Alte Garde Stellung (Old Guards Position) 65
Amiens 19
Ancre (River) 22, 25, 28, 31 - 32, 53, 64 - 66, 77, 89 – 90, 92, 126, 157
Ancre (Valley) 28, 72, 76, 109
Arras 19, 53, 61
Artilleriegraben 102
Artillerie Mulde (Artillery Hollow), Beaucourt 31, 91, 96, 137 - 138
Auchonvillers 25 - 26, 31, 33, 72, 79, 98, 118
Authuille 28
Baden 19, 35
Bangalore Torpedo 52
Bapaume 19, 20, 53, 89, 144
Battleground Europe titles
Beaucourt 15
Beaumont Hamel 15
Redan Ridge 15, 102
Serre 15
Thiepval 140
Baum Mulde (Boom Ravine) 23
Beaucourt 22, 24 - 25, 27, 69, 74, 91, 98, 106 – 107, 109, 136 - 137
Beaucourt Redoubt 64 - 65, 68, 77, 96, 136, 147, 157
Beaucourt Station 28, 69
Beaumont North Minefield 38 - 40, 118, 120
Beauregard Farm 21 - 24, 55
Below, General von 63
Bergwerk (Mine) 79, 119 - 120

Biefvillers 65, 138
British Army
Corps:
VIII 64, 75
X 64
Divisions:
4th 83
29th 48, 72, 118
31st 146
39th 89
51st (Highland) 106, 112, 118
63rd (Royal Naval) 95, 135 - 136
Regiments:
Argyll and Sutherland Highlanders 115, 118
Border 78, 102, 104
Dorsetshire 140
Essex 78
Highland Light Infantry 102
Kings Own 124, 127
King's Own Yorkshire Light Infantry 102
Lancashire Fusiliers 52, 115, 121
Newfoundland 78
Royal Fusiliers 52
Seaforth Highlanders 87
South Wales Borderers 40, 43, 78, 140
Bucquoy 146
Cambrai 19, 20, 35, 53, 144
Cemeteries
British:
Beaumont Hamel 115, 118 – 119
Frankfurt Trench 147
Hawthorn Ridge Number 1 110, 114
Hawthorn Ridge

Number 2 112
Hunter's 112
Munich Trench 131 – 132
New Munich Trench 147
Queen's 146
Redan Ridge Number 1 33, 120
Redan Ridge Number 2 118
Redan Ridge Number 3 33, 120
Serre Road Number 1 60, 126, 128
Serre Road Number 2 56, 120, 124, 127 – 128, 150
Ten Tree Alley 147
Waggon Road 131 - 132
German:
Achiet le Petit 143 - 146
Fricourt 79, 148 - 153
Labry 124, 127
Neuville St Vaast 150
Sapignies 81
Vermandovillers 150
Cirkus (Circus) 76, 106, 109, 135
Comité du Tourism de la Somme 13
Courcelette 20, 54, 140 – 141, 144
Danger Tree 113
Entenschnabel (Duck's Bill) 61
Erlenbusch, Oberst 71
Feste Alt-Wüttermberg See Beaucourt Redoubt
Feste Schwaben See Schwaben Redoubt
Feste Soden See Soden Redoubt
Feste Staufen See Stuff Redoubt
Frankfurt Trench 102

158

French Army
Second Army 57
Corps:
  XI 57
  XIV 57
Division:
  21st 57
Regiments:
  18th 24
  22nd 20
Fricourt 78
Geologengraben (Station Alley) 76 - 77, 105 – 106, 109, 135
German Army
Second Army 55, 63, 65
Corps:
  Guards 24
  I Bavarian 59, 122
  II Bavarian 19
  XIV Reserve 19, 23 - 24, 32, 40 - 41, 53, 55, 59, 62 - 63
Divisions:
  2nd Guards Reserve 132
  10th Bavarian Reserve 65
  12th 90
  26th Reserve 19, 20, 35, 46, 53 - 54, 56, 58, 63, 65, 98, 107, 120, 132, 138 – 141, 143, 151, 156
  28th Reserve 19, 55
  33rd 126
  52nd 53 - 55, 62
Brigades:
  26 Field Artillery 157
  51Reserve 65, 68, 71 – 72, 75, 88, 156 - 157
  96 Reserve 107
  185 56
Marine Infantry 143 – 144
Cavalry Regiment:
  1 150
Infantry Regiments:
  1 (Marine Infantry) 144
  5 (Bavarian) 26
  6 Guards 107
  16 (Bavarian) 65
  17 (Bavarian) 26
  23 90, 96, 98, 101 – 102, 132
  25 102
  57 107
  62 89 – 90, 92 – 93, 95 – 98, 102, 115
  63 101
  98 128
  117 117
  136 35, 107
  159 107
  169 84, 87, 101
  170 55 - 58
  173 101
  180 20 - 21, 31, 54, 56 - 57, 61, 130
  185 56, 102 - 103
  186 56
  190 56
  403 107
  413 143
Reserve Infantry Regiments:
  1 (Bavarian) 126
  6 (Bavarian) 65
  8 (Bavarian) 65
  15 101, 103 - 104
  55 89 – 90, 92 – 93, 95 – 96, 98, 136
  65 102
  95 95
  99 20, 25, 27 - 28, 30 - 31, 33, 35, 41, 53 - 54, 56, 98, 106 – 107, 140, 143, 147
  109 55 - 56
  110 25, 26 - 27, 31
  111 55, 149
  119 20, 28, 35, 40, 47 - 48, 50, 52 - 53, 56 - 59, 61, 65, 67, 70, 72, 75 – 80, 83, 85, 89, 92, 111, 113, 115, 139 – 140, 156 - 157
  120 20
  121 20, 54 - 57, 60, 65 - 66, 68 - 69, 75, 81 – 85, 90 – 91, 98, 101, 120, 125, 136, 156
  122 152
Reserve Field Artillery Regiments:
  26 21 - 22, 24 - 25, 54, 71, 138
Reserve Foot Artillery Regiment:
  10 55
Engineer Battalion:
  13 25
Grall, Oberst 23, 28, 31, 33, 106 – 107, 147
Grallsburg 64, 66 - 67, 77, 96, 102, 105 – 106, 111, 114, 132, 135, 147, 157
Grandcourt 22 - 24, 69, 81, 156
Great War Forum 13
Grévillers 65
Guillemont 89
Hamel 28 - 30, 139
Hang Stellung (Station Trench) 77, 109, 157
Hansa Stellung (Hanseatic Position) 106, 147
Hawthorn Crater 109, 114
Hawthorn Ridge 25, 28, 48 - 49, 52, 72, 75, 78, 81, 83, 93, 99, 106, 118, 120, 140
Hébuterne 63, 143
Heiden, Major 59, 61, 122

Heidenkopf (Quadrilateral)
59 - 60, 62, 68, 72, 83 –
86, 88, 101, 118, 120 –
123, 126, 129, 132
Irles   54, 135
Josenhans, Oberstleutnant
68
Kolonie (Colony) 95, 135
Kriegsministergraben 102
La Louvière Farm 56 - 57
Leiling, Hauptmann Franz
33, 35, 134
Leiling Mulde 42, 106, 111
Leiling Schlucht See Y Ravine
Leilingstollen 35, 72, 74,
106, 109, 135
Mailly   31, 52, 58, 60,
66, 83, 120, 122, 146
Marne 18
Meerscheidt-Hüllesem, Major
23, 25 - 26, 54, 56, 58, 59
Mesnil 31
Metz 19
Miraumont 21 - 23, 52, 53
- 55, 70, 135 – 136, 138
– 139, 141 – 142, 145
- 146
Musketen 79, 98, 116, 156
National Army Museum
124
Newfoundland Memorial
40, 77, 106, 109 – 111,
114, 120, 135, 147
Ovillers   33

Ovillers Spur 89
Owen, Wilfred 122
Pope's Nose 85
Poser, Oberstleutnant von
96
Pozières   20, 54
Puisieux   24, 56, 91, 146
Pys 23
Redan Ridge 25 - 26, 31,
33, 54 - 56, 61, 65 - 66,
72, 83, 89 – 90, 98, 101
– 102, 114, 132, 147
Richtofen, Rittmeister
Freiherr von 148, 150 -151
Ruined Mill (due north of
Grandcourt) 24, 54
Rupprecht, Crown Prince of
Bavaria 19
Schloss Stellung (Chateau
Position) 98, 136
Schlucht Stollen 34, 36, 111
Schwaben Redoubt 106, 147
St Pierre Divion 28, 35, 77,
85, 109 – 110, 157
Serre 24, 27, 31, 52 - 53,
55 - 56, 58 – 64, 66, 78,
83, 101, 120, 122, 126,
131 – 132, 145 – 146
Sicher, Friedrich 151
Soden, Generalleutnant
Freiherr von 46 - 47, 56,
62, 132
Soden Redoubt 54, 64, 66,
96, 99, 101, 114, 117,

130, 132
Somme Tourist Board 13
Stallmulde (Stable Hollow)
23
Station Road 35, 77, 106,
133 - 134
Steinbruch Stellung (Quarry
Position) 77, 106, 111,
132, 148, 157
Stuff Redoubt 81
Thiepval   21, 23, 65, 78,
89, 92, 147
Thiepval Memorial 109
Toutvent Farm 54 - 55
Uhland, Ludwig 151
Ulster Tower 85, 109, 147
University College, London
124
Verdun   126
Verkehrstunnel 35
Vimy   53, 150
Whitehead, Ralph 124
Wundt, Generalleutnant von
59, 65
Württemberg, King of
139, 141
Y Ravine   28, 34 - 36, 40,
44, 66, 72, 77, 85, 90,
92, 95, 106, 110, 112,
147, 157
Ziegesar, Oberstleutnant
von   67